MOVING TO ITALY

THE ULTIMATE BOOK
TO LIVE UNDER THE ITALIAN SUN

THE RULES, RATES AND INFORMATION
IN OUR GUIDES ARE CURRENT AS OF
THE PUBLICATION DATE OF THE BOOK.
WE CANNOT BE HELD RESPONSIBLE FOR ANY
ALTERATION OR MISINTERPRETATION
OF THE LAWS AND THEIR CONSEQUENCES
AFTER THE PUBLICATION OF OUR WORK.
OUR PARTNERS LAWYERS, NOTARIES AND
TAX EXPERTS PROVIDE METICULOUS
LEGAL MONITORING ALLOWING US TO HAVE
UP-TO-DATE MANUALS WITHIN THE LIMIT
OF AN ANNUAL OR EVEN MONTHLY EVOLUTION OF
THE MEASURES.

TABLE OF CONTENT

INTRODUCTION

Italy attracts more and more expatriates every year who wish to live there. Indeed, the country benefits from many advantages, notably its environment and its heritage. This country with its varied climate and landscape has almost as many inhabitants as the UK or France. Also, since 2019, Italy has put in place an advantageous tax system to attract expatriates by offering a partial exemption from income tax for a period of 5 years. Nevertheless, it would be a lie to reduce Italy to a simple tax exemption. Italy is much more than that, and expatriates who decide to move there are not mistaken.

ITALY'S CLIMATE AND LANDSCAPE: UNDENIABLE ADVANTAGES

Although the tax system is naturally an important criterion when deciding to live in Italy, the country is nonetheless full of undeniable assets, starting with the climate. It is mild almost all year round, with pronounced seasons. Italy's geographical location makes it an ideal position in the ideal position in the Mediterranean. Also the differences in climate between the North and the South are to be taken into account. It is not uncommon to have snow inland, and temperatures can exceed 40º in summer in some areas. However, the northern air brings mildness and humidity which tempers the Italian climate.

The Italian landscape is very rich and varied. This country with a history stretching back thousands of years has managed to preserve its nature in a remarkable way, and even if most of the beaches are privatised, there are still many places preserved from any human construction. From the Dolomites to Vesuvius, via Tuscany or Sardinia, Italy will delight expatriates in search of nature.

REAL ESTATE: A STILL INTERESTING MARKET

One of the other reasons why Italy is attractive is the low cost of real estate. Even though some areas have become as expensive as those found in other European metropolises, the average price of Italian property is still very attractive. There are also many villages that offer properties for 1 euro in order to revitalise depopulated town centres.

The coronavirus has also passed and prices started to fall in the second half of 2020, for the first time since 2011, almost a decade of uninterrupted price rises.

COST OF LIVING & BUDGET

The question of the budget for living in Italy is one of the first to come to mind and it is of course one of the most important. Calculating your budget for living in Italy is an important step in determining whether it is feasible or whether you should reconsider your plans. The good news is that the country has a lower cost of living than France or the UK. Of course, when you put it like that, the figure is meaningless, as the price differences depend strongly on the product category. For example:

- Fuel is as expensive as in France, with a price of €1.60 per litre in May 2019;
- Cigarettes are cheaper;
- Eating out is cheaper in the villages;
- Food is cheaper;
- Hygiene and household products are more expensive;
- Electricity is one of the most expensive in Europe and housing is poorly insulated;
- VAT is 22%.

Each expatriate will have to calculate his budget according to his different expenses.

ADMINISTRATIVE FORMALITIES

In order to move to Italy, it is necessary to complete a number of administrative formalities, some of which start well before you start packing. Therefore, each future expatriate should draw up a personal list of each service he/she will have to contact. Before leaving the country of origin, it will be necessary to contact

- Social Security ;
- Taxes;
- Utilities (water, gas, internet, electricity);
- Mutual insurance...

One of the mistakes of a "beginner" is not to find out about the possibility of cancelling subscriptions, such as the Internet, for example. Some people find themselves committed to a long term contract and have to pay 40 € per month for 2 years, and for nothing. It is therefore important to be careful to send cancellation letters in good time. The Codice Fiscale, the Italian tax number, is also the first and most important administrative step to take before leaving.

Once in Italy, you will also have a series of administrative procedures to complete in order to be able to live your expatriation in Italy with peace of mind. Anagrafe, SPID, Consular Register: there are many formalities to be completed before you can fully consider yourself an expatriate in Italy. We will discuss in detail all the steps to be taken in order to settle down without any hitch.

PREPARING YOUR MOVE: THE KEY TO A SERENE EXPATRIATION

In this guide, we will show you what you need to know in order to prepare for your move to Italy. I'm Lisbob, the expat assistant, and I'll give you the keys to a stress-free expatriation to Italy. A guide that will accompany you during your expatriation project, whether you're just thinking about it or are already packing your bags.

I am also there for you. You can contact me directly on the website www.lisbob.net: my team and I will answer all the questions that will surely come to your mind after reading this guide.

WHERE TO GO LIVE?

If you have never visited Italy before, then let us advise you to go and book a plane, train or boat ticket to come and see and feel life in Italy for yourself. The choice of the Italian region in which one decides to live is important, and Italy is a country that offers many different regions and cities that offer striking contrasts. Puglia has nothing to do with Tuscany, which is itself different from Sardinia, or even from Piedmont. What is the best region to live in Italy? What are the advantages and disadvantages as an expatriate in each Italian region? I'm Lisbob, your expat assistant, and I'll try to put together the essentials of what you need to know to live in each region of Italy. Of course, everyone has to make up their own mind when they come here, but certain trends stand out between each region. It will be up to you to discover and taste each region and, depending on your project, choose the one that will suit you best in order to be a happy expatriate.

TUSCANY

No matter what anyone says, Tuscany remains the most sought-after region in Italy for international expatriates, and for good reason. Located in the central-western part of Italy, the region of Tuscany offers unique landscapes, exceptional wines and typical farms (the famous *casolari*). Buying a property in this region is often a grail for many expats, and therefore prices are significantly more expensive compared to other equally beautiful regions, such as the Marche and Abruzzo. In addition, the region offers quality medical facilities. However it is still possible to find some good real estate deals, especially in the northern part of the region in Lunigiana. The capital of the Tuscany region, Florence, is a jewel that is constantly being discovered, but whose prices may frighten some expatriates.

Temperatures (°C)

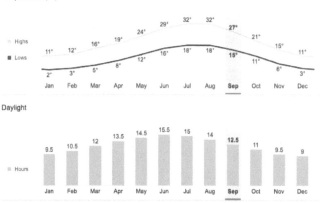

Daylight

ABRUZZO

The Abruzzo region, more commonly known as Abruzzo, is a central-southern region of Italy. With the sea to the east and the mountains to the west, Abruzzo offers a variety of landscapes and countless possibilities for visits. With its white peaked mountains and wooded hills, bordered by a turquoise sea and some of the most beautiful beaches in Europe, this is a prime area for all foreigners. Abruzzo offers a quieter, more peaceful atmosphere than other Italian regions. The pace is slower than in the big cities. Some stone villages will even make you wonder if time has stopped.

The capital of the region, L'Aquila, is sadly known for its deadly earthquake. However, affordable living costs and real estate prices are important arguments for foreigners. In addition, this region benefits from the expatriate tax program discussed later in this book.

Temperatures (°C)

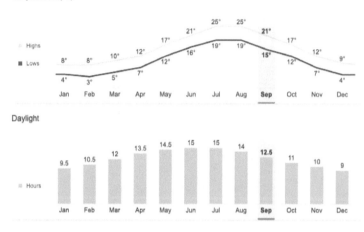

SARDINIA

The island of Sardinia is one of the most beautiful destinations in Italy. This island is 183 km long from north to south and 85 km wide at its widest point, and it offers landscapes each more splendid than the next. From its turquoise water beaches to its snow-capped mountains, Sardinia will delight all nature lovers. This region also benefits from the tax program. However, Sardinia is also full of contrasts on a social level. VIP hotels are driving up prices in some areas, while some of the less affluent cities are severely lacking in jobs and public services. Also, Sardinians are known to be rather closed to foreigners and the time and effort to integrate may be longer than elsewhere. The capital Cagliari and the second-largest city Sassari offer international flights as well as boats to connect with other major cities.

Temperatures (°C)

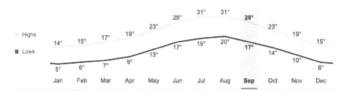

Rainfall (millimetres)

	Jan	Feb	Mar	Apr	May	Jun	Jul	Aug	Sep	Oct	Nov	Dec
	41.7	44.9	38.7	42.7	24.8	9.9	3.6	7.5	35.9	50	59.1	50.1
Days	6	6	5	6	4	1	0	1	4	5	7	7

LOMBARDY

Lombardy is an essential region of Italy. Indeed, the Lombardy region has Milan as its capital and has some of the most beautiful lakes in the world. Responsible for more than 20% of Italy's GDP, Lombardy offers the most modern health care facilities in Italy. Real estate prices are following the trend with properties being acquired for higher prices than in other regions. Be careful with the real estate criterion when making your decision. With cities such as Milan, Brescia, Bergamo and Monza, expatriates will find as many possible visits as activities to do. The lakes area (Como, Maggiore, Lugano and Iseo) will delight nature lovers and hikers, while the mountains even further north will refresh those who prefer the cold. Speaking of temperatures, they are rather cool in Lombardy, with an average maximum of 5ºC in winter and rainfall throughout the year.

Temperatures (°C)

Rainfall (millimetres)

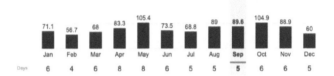

VALLE D'AOSTA

It is the region of the mountains, and also one of the most French-speaking in Italy. In fact, the Valle d'Aosta region is part of the International Association of French-speaking regions (AIRF), and French is even the official language alongside Italian. Located between Switzerland to the north and France to the west, the Valle d'Aosta region is very rich in terms of gastronomy and culture. These cheeses and hams are among the most famous in Italy and gourmet expatriates will be delighted. However, the Valle d'Aosta region is the least populated and also the least dense of all Italy. Its geography partly explains this, but also the fact that the jobs offered are mainly in the field. Agricultural and farming. Thus, in 2019, the French represented only the 5th largest expatriate population in the Valle d'Aosta region (262), a ranking dominated by Moroccans (2,065), Romanians (1,586), Albanians (825) and Tunisians (522).

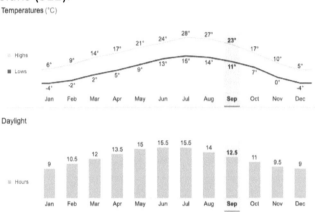

Temperatures (°C)

Daylight

SICILY

How can we talk about Italy without talking about Sicily. The largest island in the Mediterranean Sea, Sicily is also the largest region in Italy by area. This region is characterized by a strong culture and identity, which is reflected in everyday life by a certain slowness in the way of doing things, whether in administrative procedures or in cooking and weddings. Sicily also has several active volcanoes, including Etna, Stromboli and Vulcano. Because of its relief, Sicily offers a variety of landscapes and climates. In fact, there is no such thing as a Sicilian climate. Do not overlook the infamous *Sirocco* as an expatriate, an extremely hot and dry wind (40ºC) coming from the desert.

Catania is the hottest city on the island, while Palermo does not see its thermometer drop below 25ºC on summer nights. From a real estate point of view, good deals are to be found in the center of Sicily or outside the big cities of Catania and Palermo.

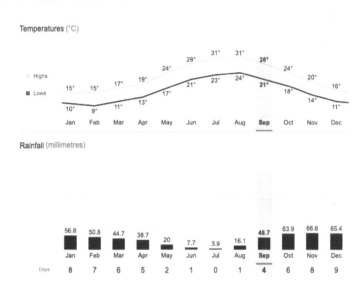

Temperatures (°C)

	Jan	Feb	Mar	Apr	May	Jun	Jul	Aug	Sep	Oct	Nov	Dec
Highs	15°	15°	17°	19°	24°	28°	31°	31°	28°	24°	20°	16°
Lows	10°	9°	11°	13°	17°	21°	23°	24°	21°	18°	14°	11°

Rainfall (millimetres)

	Jan	Feb	Mar	Apr	May	Jun	Jul	Aug	Sep	Oct	Nov	Dec
	56.8	50.8	44.7	38.7	20	7.7	3.9	16.1	48.7	63.9	66.6	65.4
Days	8	7	6	5	2	1	0	1	4	6	8	9

PIEDMONT

Ideally located with easy access to the airports of Turin and Milan, the Piedmont region is also well connected to Liguria for those who wish to be close to the sea, as the Piedmont region is located in the northern part of Italy. Close to the mainland and its neighbors, Piedmont is an excellent option for living. Famous for its magnificent vineyards classified as World Heritage Sites by UNESCO *(Langhes, Roero* and *Monferrato)* and its production of excellent wines *(Barolo, Barbera, Nebbiolo, etc.)* appreciated worldwide, the Piedmont region is surprising in many ways. The quality of life in this region is very high, and hundreds of beautiful farms are just waiting for a buyer to revive them.

Temperatures (°C)

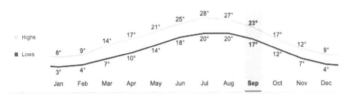

Rainfall (millimetres)

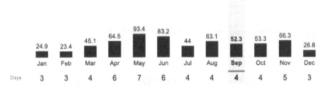

PUGLIA

Living near the sea is always a good idea, especially for those who wish to spend their expatriation in a sunny climate. Puglia is now one of the most sought-after maritime destinations in southern Italy, offering beautiful beaches and crystal-clear waters. It is a little gem recently discovered by the international community and its popularity is growing. In this area it is still possible to find reasonably priced properties, such as *masserie* and *trulli*, which are typical houses that cannot be found anywhere else.

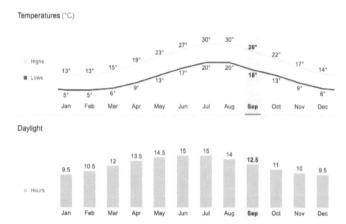

Temperatures (°C)

Highs
Lows

	Jan	Feb	Mar	Apr	May	Jun	Jul	Aug	Sep	Oct	Nov	Dec
Highs	13°	13°	15°	19°	23°	27°	30°	30°	26°	22°	17°	14°
Lows	5°	5°	6°	9°	13°	17°	20°	20°	16°	13°	9°	6°

Daylight

Hours

Jan	Feb	Mar	Apr	May	Jun	Jul	Aug	Sep	Oct	Nov	Dec
9.5	10.5	12	13.5	14.5	15	15	14	12.5	11	10	9.5

ADVANTAGES AND INCOVENIENTS

Despite the fact that Italy has many assets to attract expatriates from all over the world, the fact remains that the country of the Renaissance has quite strong contrasts in some areas with its European neighbours, particularly in terms of integration. Everyone will find advantages and disadvantages and as the saying goes, tastes and colours....

ADVANTAGES:

- **Weather: Italy's weather is generally sunny and allows you to enjoy the outdoors for most of the year. However, some expatriates should be aware that in some regions of Italy, summers can be very hot (Puglia, Sicily), and winters very cold and wet (Lombardy, Valle d'Aosta). It should not**

be forgotten that Italy is a country that receives several types of climate.

- **Heritage & Lifestyle** : Italy is an extremely rich country in terms of culture, traditions and culture. Thanks to a good conservation and development of its heritage, Italy has no reason to be ashamed when it comes to monuments, museums and other places to visit, vestiges of its Greek, Roman and Renaissance past. Rome is a capital to which it seems all roads lead, the Vatican is the spiritual centre of Christianity, and cities like Milan, Florence and Venice are world famous for their heritage. One thing is for sure, living in Italy you will never be bored.

- **Health**: Italy has very good doctors and hospital universities. In fact, the country is often ranked among the best in the world in terms of public health care, as evidenced by the life expectancy of Italians, which is also linked to their diet. However, the public health care system in Italy suffers from a shortage of both staff and funds. It is not uncommon to have to wait several months for a consultation and many foreigners are surprised by this system. Private health insurance will be recommended in order to save time and peace of mind. This is discussed in more detail later in the book.

INCONVENIENTS

- **Contrasts**: Northern Italy is not Southern Italy, and even more so since the economic crisis of 2008. Indeed, Italy has very strong contrasts between a separatist and rich North and a poor and more traditional South. This is reflected in the infrastructure and public services, but also in the relations between Italians themselves and foreigners. This may come as a surprise to some, but a Sicilian will not easily make friends with a Lombard, any more than with a Frenchman. So before deciding where to live, you should consider all the criteria.

- **Language**: When you are growing up, learning a new language may not be a priority. Indeed, it is understandable to be less motivated by the idea of having to "go back to school" and start from scratch with a new language. The beginner's mistake is to think that Italian and others European languages are almost similar, but when spoken, the difference will be immediately apparent and many expatriates may be put off by the difficulty of understanding the Italian accent. In addition, some regions have a local dialect which will complicate matters further. Take heart though, the Latin roots will make Italian easier to learn for us than Chinese.

- **Integration**: Italians are not known for being the most welcoming people in the world. Indeed, Italian regions have more autonomy than in other European countries and the defence of traditions is more present than elsewhere. This defence will be felt in the relationship that Italians have with what is foreign in the broadest sense. This should not be seen as aggressiveness or mistrust, but as a barrier to what could harm their culture. However, this barrier to integration may put many people off. Learning some basic Italian or local dialect will be a good start.

9 ADMINISTRATIVE PROCEDURES AND FORMALITIES

When expatriating to a new country, a certain number of administrative steps must be taken in order to fully settle in and become an expatriate. This is even more true in Italy where different authorities issue different important documents, and where it is sometimes difficult to do the administrative steps in the right order. Procedures to become a resident, tax identification number, pet registration, car registration, there are many compulsory steps for those who want to live in Italy and it is not easy to know how to live in Italy and be in order. Moving to Italy entails a number of obligations towards the various government agencies and it is important to be in order to avoid any worries and to complete all the necessary formalities. Any self-respecting expatriate must take these administrative steps in order to settle down fully. What are the administrative formalities and steps to take to live in Italy? How to be in order and respect the steps to register to live in Italy? I tell you everything about the administrative steps to take when you decide to live in Italy.

CODICE FISCALE - ITALIAN TAX NUMBER

The tax number is called Codice Fiscale and it is the identification number for the tax authorities in Italy.

Everyone has one, even babies, and it is a mandatory step to access many services, such as registering at the health center or opening a bank account. This is simply the first step on the list of administrative procedures and formalities to do in order to live in Italy. If you apply for it before moving to Italy, the Italian tax identification number Codice Fiscale can be obtained from the Italian Consulate in your home town, with proof of identity. If you want to apply for it after you have moved to Italy, you have to go to an office of the Agenzia delle Entrate in your place of residence. This is an administrative process that Lisbob can do for you.

The Codice Fiscal number is important because it identifies you from a fiscal point of view and it is compulsory to open a bank account, to subscribe to a gas or electricity contract, or to buy a cell phone.

This is a process that I explain in detail in a dedicated chapter.

REGISTRATION IN THE CIVIL REGISTRY - ANAGRAFE

This is one of the most important administrative procedures when moving to Italy. Registration in Anagrafe, the Italian civil status registry, is mandatory for anyone who resides in Italy for more than 3 months. To register with the Civil Status Registry, Anagrafe, you must go to the town hall of your municipality of residence to file an application for registration with the Civil Status Registry, Anagrafe.

Documents required to apply for registration in the Civil Registry in Italy:

-   Valid identity document;
-   Document certifying the applicant's work in Italy (if the application is made in the professional context): employee (employment contract with a company) or self-employed (registration with a chamber of commerce or VAT number);
-   Document attesting to enrollment in educational or vocational training courses (if stay and registration are required for study or training purposes): certificate of enrollment in a recognized public or private institution;
-   Certificate of financial capacity to support yourself and your family;
-   Certificate of health insurance policy or other appropriate coverage for all risks in the national territory.

Once the file has been completed and handed over to the Italian authorities, you must wait for the local police to carry out the necessary checks. Following this visit, you will be issued a certificate of residency, and you will then officially become an Italian resident.

SUBSCRIBING TO THE ITALIAN SOCIAL PROTECTION SYSTEM

One of the most important steps when settling in Italy is to be able to benefit from access to the Italian social protection system. The Italian social security is called Servizio Sanitario Nazionale. Membership in the SSN is certified by a magnetic card called Tessera Sanitaria or Tessera Europea di Assicurazione Malattia (TEAM) which is in fact the European Health Insurance Card.

This card is necessary to carry out all health-related procedures and to receive health care within the framework of the social protection system. For example, the Tessera Sanitaria is essential to buy medicines and treatments in the pharmacy or to go to the hospital. In order to obtain it, you must go to an office of the Aziende Sanitarie Locali (ASL, local health companies) once you have registered for the SSN, and ask for the Tessera Sanitaria or the TEAM card.

OPEN A BANK ACCOUNT

Among the steps and formalities to be done in order to live in Italy, opening a bank account in Italy is one of the first steps to be taken when moving to Italy. Indeed, the opening of a bank account allows you to domicile your income and to benefit from banking services such as debit or credit cards, home loans or international transfers. This is an administrative process that Lisbob can do for you.

The bank account cannot be opened without a TIN in Italy. It is also necessary to present documents in order to open an account, such as
- Identification: valid national identity card or passport;
- Codice Fiscale;
- Proof of address: electricity, water or telephone bill;

- Proof of occupation: employment contract, pay slip.

PETS

If you decide to move to Italy with your pet then you will need to make certain arrangements for your four-legged friend and follow certain steps. In fact, Italy, like other European countries, imposes certain regulations for pets and the ones you will take with you when you move to Italy will not escape them.

In Italy the registration and the license of authorization are compulsory for all dogs from 3 to 6 months old. The registration of a pet must be done at the City Hall of the area of residence of the owner or keeper of the animal.

In order to proceed with the registration and obtain the license for your pet in Italy, you will need to present:

- Animal health bulletin (rabies vaccine up to date)

- Electronic identification chip

Some breeds of dogs fall into special categories and require special procedures and formalities.

REGISTRATION OF CHILDREN IN SCHOOL

When moving to Italy with your family, it is important to find out in advance about your children's or grandchildren's schooling and the registration process. As a foreigner, there are different possibilities to enroll your children in school.

- Italian public or private school: it is determined according to your residence and it will be necessary to register your child there;
- French school: there are a total of 6 French schools in Italy, mainly in the big cities: Rome, Milan, Naples, Florence and Turin. Budgets range from €3,500 to €5,000 per year per student for tuition;
- International school: the teaching is generally in English, and the prices are higher: it will be necessary to count between 9,000 and €14,000 per year and per pupil;

The choice of schooling for your children will depend greatly on your expatriation project: its duration, its purpose, as well as your personal aspirations. For a better integration, the Italian public education system is recommended.

GET THE SPID

Administrative procedures have been modernized and simplified in recent years. In order to pay taxes or fines, for example, it is necessary to obtain a SPID.

It is a system that allows you to identify yourself online and to do administrative procedures without having to move. I will explain in detail how to apply for it and how to get it.

CAR REGISTRATION

This is one of the most important points to consider when deciding to move to Italy and one of the most complicated steps to take. Taking your car, or selling it before leaving? This is not a trivial issue. Indeed, the steps can be complicated and the taxes can become high. You will have more information by using our simulator in order to be more serene in these steps and administrative formalities.

Nevertheless, it is important to register your car in the right order and with all the documents. In fact, too many foreign car owners have been forced to pay unexpected taxes or take their car to the impound lot because of a missing document, a misunderstood step or a wrongly filled out form and a missed deadline.

Let the professionals do it for you: some companies do everything for you, from registering your car to applying for tax exemption.

DRIVER'S LICENSE EXCHANGE

You have a driving license with no administrative validity and are a resident in Italy. Did you know that you have to exchange your French driving license for an Italian one after two years of residence? In fact, the pink license will no longer be recognized by the Italian authorities and you must start the process to exchange it for an Italian license.

Be careful because if you are checked with a French driving license that is not valid in the eyes of the Italian authorities, you risk fines of up to €3,000, and greater worries in the event of an accident where you are at fault!

To exchange your driver's license for an Italian one you can read our article on the subject. This is an administrative process that others can do for you.

We have done a tour of the administrative procedures and formalities to do to live in Italy. However, as each expatriation is different, certain steps are not included in this article. You can contact Lisbob and his team for more information about other formalities to live in Italy.

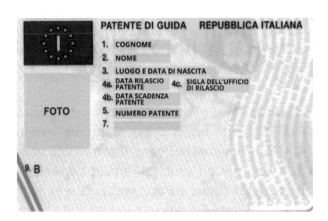

PATENTE DI GUIDA   REPUBBLICA ITALIANA

1. COGNOME
2. NOME
3. LUOGO E DATA DI NASCITA
4a. DATA RILASCIO PATENTE   4c. SIGLA DELL'UFFICIO DI RILASCIO
4b. DATA SCADENZA PATENTE
5. NUMERO PATENTE
7.

FOTO

9. B

41

NEW TAX STATUS

Will Italy replace Portugal in the hearts of European expatriates? Portugal offers a tax status for expatriates called NHR, Non-Habitual Resident. It allows you to benefit from a 10% tax rate on your retirement pensions for 10 years. This NHR tax status attracts many retirees and other countries are interested in doing the same. Italy, supported by its new government, has decided to take the plunge and set up an advantageous tax status to attract European expatriates. Some differences with Portugal, the tax base will be reduced by 90% and it will be necessary to live in the southern regions of Italy, including Sardinia, and in cities of less than 20,000 inhabitants. What is the tax status in Italy? What are the conditions to benefit from it? I tell you all about this new tax status in Italy.

A TAX STATUS COMPETING WITH THAT OF A NON-HABITUAL RESIDENT IN PORTUGAL

Italy has decided to introduce a new tax status to attract European expatriates. This status clearly competes with the non-habitual resident status found in Portugal. As a reminder, in Portugal the NHR status allows retirees to benefit from a total tax exemption for 10 years. To be able to benefit from it, 2 conditions must be met:

- Not having been a tax resident for the 5 years preceding the application;
- Have a private pension.

This tax status attracts many French and European retirees every year, who come to enjoy, in addition to the sun and security, a very significant tax advantage. This system even makes some people jealous among the Portuguese population who see it as unfair competition. In fact, some political parties are making the end of NHR status and Golden Visa a social justice priority for the next election.

Italy has recently had a new government which, after long negotiations with Brussels, has decided to apply a fiscal policy aimed at developing the southern regions of Italy, which are poorer and less developed than the northern regions.

These regions are as follows: Sicily, Calabria, Campania, Puglia, Sardinia, Molise, Basilicata and Abruzzo. They hope to attract Italian retirees who have left the country and also those from other European neighbours, just like the NHR status in Portugal, which is still attracting European retirees and is accused of 'unfair tax competition' by some of its neighbours.

Here are the regions that are affected by this new tax status in Italy:

Regions where 7% tax is applied

CONDITIONS

Many countries criticize Portugal for applying a 0% tax rate on certain foreign income, and it is often this point that comes up in discussions about whether or not to be taxed and in which country. France, for example, considers that one cannot not be taxed, and that if you are not taxed in Portugal, then you must be taxed in France, the country of origin of the pensions.

Italy seems to have found the answer by applying a low rate of **7%**. The conditions to be able to benefit from it are the following:

- Living in a region of **southern** Italy: Sicily, Calabria, Campania, Puglia, Sardinia, in Molise, Basilicata or in Abruzzo;

- Settling in a city of less than **20,000** inhabitants;
- Receive income from a European country.

These conditions, different from the NHR status in Portugal, are implemented since January 1, 2019. Italy hopes to attract European expatriates and boost the southern regions and the island of Sardinia. This tax competition between European countries and the greater mobility of foreigners allows Italy to offer a different status than the NHR in Portugal, but with other advantages. With the revenue from this tax system, Italy intends to finance the universities of these regions, which are depopulated and in greater economic difficulty than the North.

ITALIAN INCOME TAX RATES, BRACKETS AND SCALES

In Italy, almost all income is subject to income tax. The Italian Revenue Agency, also known as *Agenzia delle Entrate*, sends an income statement to taxpayers every year, which they must complete and send. Tax returns must be filed online by October 2, or on paper between May 2 and June 30. We distinguish the same categorical incomes as in other countries:

- Earned income (wages, salaries, self-employed income),

- Benefits in kind, pensions (retirement, food),

- Property income,

- Capital gains,

- Family property income,

- Dividends

Italy has 5 tax brackets in its progressive scale :

Up to €15,000 - 23%
From €15,000 to €28,000 - 27%
From €28,000 to €55,000 - 38%
From €55,000 to €75,000 - 41%
Above €75,000 - 43%

HOW TO OBTAIN A CODICE FISCALE

When you decide to live in Italy, there are some steps that are essential. Obtaining an Italian tax number, called Codice Fiscale, is part of this. It is a number that is assigned to every person living in Italy, expatriate or not, and allows the Italian tax authorities to identify any Italian or foreign citizen. This Italian Codice Fiscale allows you to work, open a bank account or buy a house in Italy: it is therefore a fundamental step for any expat living in Italy. This unique and personal combination of numbers and letters can sometimes become complicated to obtain if one is not prepared for the administrative procedures. What is an Italian tax code and what is it used for? How do I get a tax number in Italy? Lisbob, your expatriate assistant in Italy, is going to tell you everything about the Italian Codice Fiscale.

WHAT IS AN ITALIAN CODICE FISCALE?

The Codice Fiscale is the Italian national identification number for taxes. It is a unique and personal combination of letters and numbers that identifies any Italian or foreign citizen at all times. The Italian tax authorities provide a credit card with the tax number on it.

Example of the Italian tax code for Italian citizens (Codice Fiscale):

The Codice Fiscale (Italian tax number) is issued directly by the Agenzia delle Entrate (Italian Tax Agency). However, since it can be calculated from personal information (full name, date and place of birth), it is not considered private or confidential, nor is it recognized as official proof of identity. Also, it does not contain an image of the holder (unlike any other valid ID).

WHAT CAN I DO WITH MY ITALIAN CODICE FISCALE?

Having an Italian tax number does not mean that you have to pay taxes as such, but this Codice Fiscale is necessary in order to:
- Register with the Italian National Health Service (SSN - Servizio Sanitario Nazionale);

- Open a bank account;
- Collect a payment;
- Receive a tax refund;
- Rent or buy a house;
- Or even just buy a SIM card/cell phone.

The tax code can be used either by showing the card or by directly typing the alphanumeric number located on the front of the card into the payment terminal.

HOW TO GET A CODICE FISCALE IN ITALY?

There are two ways to obtain your Codice Fiscale (Italian tax number).

BEFORE YOUR DEPARTURE

It is **strongly** recommended to ask for your Codice Fiscale **before** leaving for Italy.

Indeed, having it in advance allows you to make other steps and to arrive serenely in Itaile, like finding an accommodation or a job more quickly. Many expatriates have waited for a job offer or a successful apartment visit to begin the process. Result: the job or apartment of your dreams passes you by.

In order to obtain the Italian Codice Fiscale you just have to fill in the _registration form_ in less than 2 minutes. Our team will process your request and you will get your tax code within a few working days, entirely remotely! No need to travel, and you save time and money.

Of course, this Codice Fiscale is valid throughout Italy and is definitive.

Advantages of requesting the Codice Fiscale online:
- No travel
- Be able to take other steps before arriving (work, housing, etc.)
- Most important step to take to live in Italy
- 24/7 service

WHEN YOU'RE THERE

It is also possible to request it in Italy, although this is more complicated. You will need a valid identity document (either your passport or an identity card issued by the municipality of residence). If your passport is lost or stolen, you can ask your local embassy to issue you an emergency passport. Otherwise, you can show your valid residence permit or the notice of receipt of the application for a residence permit.

In order to obtain a tax code in Italy, you must present
- Identity document
- Form AA4/8 completed and signed
- Photocopy of identity document

It is possible to find and print the AA4/8 form directly on the website of the Agenzia delle Entrate (the form and the instructions are in English).

If you don't have a printer, you can email the pdf file to one of the many 'fotocopisteria' and let them print it for you. You can also find a copy at the office of the Agenzia delle Entrate, but Lisbob advises you to prepare the form in advance. Then you must make a copy of your ID (some offices require it) and bring it to the nearest office of the Agenzia delle Entrate.

Here are the steps to follow to obtain an Italian Codice Fiscale:
- Print and fill out form AA4/8;
- Make a copy of your ID;
- Go to an Agenzia delle Entrate;
- Take a ticket;
- Receive your Codice Fiscale card at home.

You will receive the plastic Codice Fiscale card later (within a few days or probably within a few weeks) only if you have not requested an Italian health insurance card (Tessera Sanitaria) at the same time. If you have applied for an Italian health insurance card, you will only receive this one. Don't worry: it will contain both your health insurance number and your Italian tax code.

In the end, if you decide to use the Codice Fiscale to register with the Italian National Health Service (SSN - Servizio Sanitario Nazionale), the Italian health insurance card

(Tessera Sanitaria) replaces the Codice Fiscale card. The Italian health insurance card (Tessera Sanitaria) will have the same validity period as your residence permit, while the Codice Fiscale does not expire because it remains the same for your entire life. However, since the Italian health insurance card (Tessera Sanitaria) and the tax code are on the same card, you can still use it even if the Italian health insurance card expires.

If you are not yet an expatriate in Italy, you can apply for a codice fiscale directly from your home country at any Italian consulate. If you are entering the country on a work visa then you already have an Italian tax number. This is issued together with the visa by the Italian diplomatic representatives or consulates abroad.

HOW TO BUY A PROPERTY

Buying a house in Italy is just as or more complicated than in other European countries. New language, new rules, it is important to learn about the process of buying real estate beforehand so as not to be surprised. Many expatriates have rushed in believing they had found the right deal and have found themselves in complicated situations. From the search for the property to the signature, through the accompaniment, I have listed all the steps to acquire a property in Italy. I'm Lisbob, the expat assistant, and I'm going to tell you how to buy a house in Italy.

CHOICE OF LOCATION AND VISITS

This is perhaps the most enjoyable part of buying a home in Italy: visiting properties and making your choice. Nevertheless, it is important to take advantage of these visits and their preparation in order not to waste time and to be sure to find a property which corresponds to you. Determine what you are looking for by first identifying the area(s) you are interested in and the type of property you are looking for. A retirement home will be very different from a vacation home or a downtown apartment. We will also need to ask ourselves questions such as
- Are you planning to have guests?
- Do you want to be close to an airport?

- A hospital?
- Do you plan to use your car regularly?
- Would you like to meet other expatriates?

These are obvious questions, but they are often forgotten by future expatriates, and they can change the search results. By explaining exactly what you want, the real estate agent will find it easier to find the ideal property.

OBTAIN THE ITALIAN TAX NUMBER (CODICE FISCALE).

The Codice Fiscale is the Italian tax number. It is mandatory to buy a property in Italy. Not only will you need it when you make your purchase, but you will also need it when you open a bank account, buy insurance, purchase a car or deal with the tax authorities. Many expatriates fail to ask for it before starting the real estate purchase process, and deadlines for the sale agreement are missed because of the delay in obtaining it.

I advise you to ask for the Codice Fiscale before your departure in Italy for the visits. It can be obtained online, directly on our website or app.

This way, you will already have what you need and will not risk losing your deposit.

STUDY AND EVALUATION

As in other countries, it is strongly advised to obtain a survey and appraisal on a property that interests you. Make sure that you are not paying too much for the property in question and that you check the condition of the property. Also, the intended use is important, as is the possibility of doing work it.

PROPERTY RESEARCH

You can instruct your attorney to ensure that the seller actually owns the property, that the property is properly registered and has the proper building permit, and that all encumbrances on the property are fully disclosed. In Italy the notary will carry out these checks at the end of the process, just before the signing of the title deed, but it is essential that these searches are also carried out before the contract is signed and a deposit is paid in order to avoid any unpleasant surprises.

PURCHASE CONTRACT (COMPROMESSO) AND DEPOSIT (CAPARRA CONFIRMATORIA)

The research is positive? Perfect, a contract must then be drawn up, equivalent to a sales agreement. This is signed between the parties and a deposit is paid. This commits the current owner of the property to sell to the buyer, and it commits the buyer to purchase the property on the agreed upon terms. If the buyer withdraws then he loses his deposit. If the seller withdraws, the buyer may receive double the deposit.

The *Compromesso* must specify the conditions of purchase (price, down payment, what is included in the price, date of signature of the title, etc.).

PREPARE A POWER OF ATTORNEY IF NECESSARY

In Italy the signing of the title deeds is done before a notary public. This must be done on Italian territory. If the buyer cannot physically attend the signing before the notary public, it is possible to give a power of attorney to another person. The signed power of attorney confirms that the person has been authorized to do certain things on behalf of the buyer - in this case, sign the deeds.

SIGNING THE TITLE DEEDS (ROGITO)

This is the big moment: the signing of the title deeds between the buyer and seller (or their representatives via a power of attorney) before a notary public. The two parties physically meet in front of the notary to sign the new deeds. Just before doing so, the notary must do some last-minute research to ensure that the property is still registered in the seller's name and to identify any encumbrances on the property. This is a last-minute check to avoid scams and other disappointments.

REGISTER THE PROPERTY AND PAY THE TAXES

Nw you have a property in Italy! Once the title deed is signed, the purchase must be registered with the Italian Land Registry and the corresponding real estate taxes paid. The taxes to be paid vary depending on the type of purchase (first-time buyer or reseller), the value of the property, and also whether the property will be your permanent residence or not. This is discussed in a separate chapter.

MAKING AN ITALIAN WILL

It makes sense at this point to make an Italian will to ensure that your wishes are respected in the event of your death. In August 2015, a European directive came into effect. This means that the laws of the country of residence apply to all assets, not the law of nationality. That is unless a will was made to cover the assets in this country. This is a point I will address in another chapter.

You now know the main steps to acquire a property in Italy. Don't forget that the support of a professional who speaks your language will be an essential asset in order not to fall into the most common traps. It is unfortunately common as an expatriate to come across unscrupulous people who will not hesitate to try to rob you, as in other countries.

You can consult our professional directory to find real estate agents, lawyers or notaries who can help you with the process of buying a property in Italy.

REAL ESTATE TAXATION

Before buying a house or a property in Italy, it is essential to understand the different rules and calculations regarding real estate taxes to which everyone is subject. Indeed, many expatriates buy a property unprepared and, once they own a house in Italy, receive tax notices that they had not anticipated. The rules and calculations of taxes are different depending on where you live, how many houses you own and other factors. Also, a good preparation is essential concerning the taxes of your house in Italy and this well before any decision of purchase. What are the real estate taxes in Italy? How do you calculate real estate taxes? Here's a list of taxes in Italy, step by step.

TAXES WHEN BUYING A PROPERTY

VAT

When buying a house in Italy, there are some tax aspects to keep in mind. Indeed, the taxes to be paid are different depending on whether you buy a house from a real estate developer or from a private individual.

The purchase and sale of real estate through construction or renovation companies, with the exception of special cases, are subject to VAT, which is payable directly to the seller.

Also, it will be necessary to take into account whether the purchase of the property can benefit from the recognition of 'first home'. The purchase of the first home by an individual also allows for tax benefits if the following conditions are met:

- The buyer does not have any real rights (full ownership, usufruct, or bare ownership) on other real estate in the same city as the real estate intended for his or her first home;
- He is not already the owner of another property in Italy purchased with the tax benefit reserved for the first home;
- He/she must transfer his/her main residence to the property in question or to the city where it is located within 18 months of the purchase;
- The property must not be classified in the following cadastral categories: A1, A8 and A9 (luxury homes and villas).

The VAT rate to be applied on the sale price will be

- 10% in the absence of primary housing benefits;
- 4% in the case of a first home.

NOTARY FEES

In the case of a purchase subject to Italian VAT, the following taxes must also be paid to the notary, who will then pay them to the Tax Agency (Agenzia delle Entrate):

- Registration Fee: 200 euros;
- Mortgage Tax: 200 euros;
- Cadastral tax: 200 euros.

If you are buying a house directly from a private individual, the registration, mortgage and license fees are paid by the buyer to the Italian Notary, who will in turn pay them to the Tax Agency (Agenzia delle Entrate) when registering the property in the various registers.

Here are the notary fees for a property purchased directly from a private individual and in the absence of a 'first home' benefit:

- Registration Fee: 9%;
- Mortgage Tax: 50 euros;
- Cadastral tax: 50 euros.

The tax rates are normally applied to the current reported sales price. In case of transfer of residential properties to natural persons, the buyer can request the payment of the registration tax on the 'cadastral value' of the property. The minimum amount of the tax is always €1,000.

Here are the notary fees for a property purchased directly from a private individual and in the presence of 'first home' benefits:

- Registration Fee: 2%;
- Mortgage Tax: 50 euros;
- Cadastral tax: 50 euros.

The tax rates are also applied to the current reported sales price. In case of transfer of residential properties to natural persons, the buyer of the property can request the payment of the registration tax (Imposta di Registro) on the 'cadastral value' of the property, regardless of the actual amount of the sale price, even if it is higher than this value. The minimum amount of the tax is also €1,000.

REAL ESTATE TAXES

TASI - MUNICIPAL TAX FOR INDIVISIBLE SERVICES (TRIBUTO PER I SERVIZI INDIVISIBILI)

The TASI (Tributo per i servizi indivisibili) allows municipal administrations to take charge of the maintenance of common and public services. These services include, for example, the maintenance of green spaces, the lighting of public places and roads, the cleaning of public places and all other services that are provided equally to all citizens.

Since 2016 real estate used as a primary residence is completely exempted from the TASI regulation, with the exception, however, of luxury properties included in cadastral categories A/1, A/8, A/9. In order to calculate the TASI, various factors such as the location of the property and other coefficients must be taken into account. The advice of a specialist will be essential to calculate the total cost of this tax on indivisible services in advance.

IMU - IMPOSTA MUNICIPALE PROPRIA (SINGLE MUNICIPAL TAX)

This tax is a bit special because it is not applied to the owner's first property. The IMU, Unique Municipal Tax, must still be paid if the main house is considered a 'luxury category'. This category means that the property is registered in the cadastre under one of the following cadastral categories: A/1, A/8 and A/9, respectively mansions, villas and castles.

This tax replaced the ICI (Communal Property Tax) as well as part of the IRPEF (Individual Income Tax). The different tax rates of the IMU are chosen each year independently by each Italian municipality. Of course, they must respect the limits set by the Italian national legislation. The rates are therefore different for each local authority, and special discounts and exemptions are provided. It is therefore necessary to get information on a case-by-case basis depending on the municipality in which you wish to settle and your family situation.

CANONE RAI - AUDIOVISUAL LICENSE FEE

In Italy, as in other countries, there is a visual fee to finance public television. Owning a television is taxed, and the particularity is that this tax is deducted every month from your electricity bill. The amount of this Italian audiovisual fee does not depend on the number of television sets in the household, but only on the actual presence of a set. A homeowner with multiple audiovisual devices will not see an increase in tax. The amount of this tax is 10 monthly payments of 9 euros each.

There are 2 cases of exemption from the audiovisual fee: being over 75 years old, or not owning a television. Please note that you have to apply for this, otherwise the tax will continue to be deducted.

TARI - TAX ON HOUSEHOLD WASTE (TASSA SUI RIFIUTI)

It is this tax that keeps the streets clean. In fact, the TARI (Tassa sui rifiuti) is a tax destined to finance the collection and recycling of household waste. This tax is managed locally, directly by the various Italian municipalities. Every owner of premises or open space for any purpose that is likely to generate municipal or similar waste and the surface area of which lies wholly or mainly within the City shall pay this fee.

CAPITAL GAINS TAX ON A SALE

The capital gain realized on the sale of a property in Italy is taxed like any other income, at the marginal tax rate. There are, however, 3 exceptions to this tax:

- Sale of primary residence;
- Sale of a property possessed for more than 5 years;
- Property received by inheritance.

There is also an alternative solution to income tax. In fact, in Italy it is possible to choose a flat tax of 20% to be paid through the notary who certifies the deed of sale of the property in question.

RENTAL INCOME

As a property owner in Italy, you may be tempted to rent it out. This rental income will, of course, be taxed. This tax is called the Cedolare Secca. This is a tax regime designed for property owners in Italy that provides two types of rates. This depends on whether the owner wishes to rent out his property on the open market or with an agreed rent.

Rental annuities may be taxed as income at the marginal rate and on a taxable basis of 95% of the gross annual rental payments. It is also important to take into account the registration fees. Indeed, these fees represent a cost of 2% of the gross annual rent on the property. As for the tax on real estate capital gains, there is an alternative solution: choose a flat tax *(Cedola Secca)* of 21% of the gross annual rents on 100% of them. The owner who chooses this solution has no registration fee to pay.

5 MISTAKES YOU SHOULD AVOID MAKING WHEN BUYING A HOUSE OR A PROPERTY

Are you an expatriate in Italy looking for the house of your dreams, the one that will accommodate your entire happy family? Or are you simply looking to invest in real estate in Italy and make a profit? There are many reasons to buy a house in Italy, and many mistakes to avoid. Indeed, many expatriates have rushed to buy their property in Italy and unfortunately had to face many difficulties, and sometimes significant financial losses. House seized after purchase, wrong estimation of real estate taxes, you have to be careful when buying a house or a property in Italy. What are the pitfalls to avoid when buying a property? What are the 5 mistakes not to make? Lisbob accompanies you in this wonderful adventure. Here are the 5 mistakes not to make when buying a house or property in Italy.

NOT DOING THE NECESSARY CHECKS

Have you found the perfect home in Italy? Do not fall into the trap of not making the necessary verifications concerning the situation of the property in question from an urbanistic and cadastral point of view. In fact, it is always necessary to make sure that the property respects all the Italian laws concerning building permits for example, especially in the purchase of properties with a swimming pool, well or cabin. It is also necessary to verify that the property is authorized to receive the intended use. In order to avoid these problems, it is always necessary to check the original title deeds: in Italy one of the problems is the donation of real estate which can, in some cases, be revoked by the beneficiaries as well as the heirs. Another problem in Italy is the lack of full ownership of the property on the part of the seller and the existence of mortgages on the property.

NOT CHECKING FOR MORTGAGES

Buying a house in **Italy** doesn't have to be a nightmare. To avoid unpleasant surprises, consider asking your notary to verify that the current owner of the house you wish to acquire has no debts and that no mortgage has been placed on your future residence. This check is essential, for the peace of mind it will give you and for the hassle it will save you! A house pledged and it is your dream of living in Italy that flies away.

You can also go to a tax office to find out about the possible mortgage on your property in Italy, but this will involve long waiting hours. In the end, the notarial solution appears to be the most appropriate.

FORGETTING TO CALCULATE TAXES IN ADVANCE

When you buy a house in Italy, in addition to the price of your property, you have to pay not only the notary fees and the various administrative procedures, but also the taxes on the property purchase. The payment of these taxes is mandatory and you risk heavy fines if you do not pay them. It is strongly advised not to underestimate the impact of these taxes when purchasing your property as it can impact your budget.

You will have to pay the following Italian real estate taxes:
- Cadastral taxes;
- Registration taxes (if the property is second-hand);
- VAT (IVA in Italian) if the property is new;
- Mortgage tax (about 2% of the amount of the property).

Each of these taxes has its own method of calculation, with different coefficients in different regions of Italy. Not paying attention to these taxes when searching for a property is already a serious mistake, as the amounts can represent a good percentage of the property's value.

NOT NEGOTIATING YOUR MORTGAGE

There are two options when it comes to choosing a mortgage to buy a home in Italy. On the one hand, you can take out a fixed-rate mortgage, and on the other, a variable-rate mortgage. Each has its advantages and disadvantages. The variable-rate mortgage is less expensive than the fixed rate mortgage but has more risks. With this type of mortgage, your bank indexes your interest rate to the European EURIBOR index (one of the main money market reference rates in the euro zone). This means that they can decide to lower your interest rate when things are going well, but they can also decide to raise it when things are not! This was one of the reasons for the subprime crisis in the United States, and it is a gamble that, over the long term, can prove risky. If you're not a gambler at heart, a fixed-rate mortgage will cost you a little more, but you'll know in advance exactly how much you'll have to pay back at the end of your mortgage. It is normal in Italy to see periods of fixed-rate mortgages for only a limited time (2, 4, 6, 10, 15 years), the rest of the period being again at variable rates.

What is certain is that you should not buy a house in Italy without first negotiating your mortgage. This is a big purchase and you can make real savings by competing with other banks to get as low a price on your mortgage as possible.

THINKING YOU CAN DO EVERYTHING ON YOUR OWN

Buying a house in Italy is an extremely important step in your expatriation. So don't take the risk of getting it wrong. Lisbob is here to accompany you throughout your settlement in your new adopted country. Practical advice, opening gas and electricity contracts, and all the administrative procedures. Lisbob and their team will take care of everything, so don't hesitate to contact them in order to make your dream of expatriation to Italy a reality.

RENTING AN APARTMENT OR A HOUSE

Italy has been seducing expatriates for decades with its legendary food, wine, history, architecture, beaches and natural landscape. Thanks to certain cities, areas and tourist attractions, this Mediterranean country has a reputation for being rather expensive in terms of real estate, but these rumors are largely false. Indeed, the average cost of a one-bedroom apartment in a large city center is about €600 per month. Even in the most popular cities for expats, such as Milan, Rome and Naples, it is easy to find a comfortable one-bedroom apartment in the city center for less than €1000. In addition, if you plan to live outside of a major city, the cost of living is likely to be much more reasonable than it is in other European capitals. Whether you are looking to move to Italy for its beautiful countryside, to start your own business, or for your retirement, one of the biggest obstacles may be finding an apartment to rent or share. The time to find the ideal property to buy, renting is the ideal temporary solution. Lisbob will guide you through the most important points to know when you start your rental search. How to find an apartment or a house to rent in Italy? What are the rental rules for real estate leases? What are the documents and conditions to rent a property in Italy? I will tell you everything you need to know about renting.

REAL ESTATE AGENTS OR BROKERS

The Italian real estate market is a bit different, as most apartments are rented directly by their owners. It is quite rare to have entire buildings of rented apartments or companies with a large number of rental properties. As a result, most private landlords choose to work with an agent or broker to manage the lease negotiation, rather than spending their time managing the lease themselves.

So, you might be lucky to find an apartment online or through word of mouth that you can rent directly to the owner. This will save on agency fees, but if you want to be on the safe side and possibly get a better price, it is best to work with a real estate agent. To go directly with a landlord when you don't master the language or the rules in force is to run the risk of committing yourself to an adventure that may not be worth the effort with a poorly drafted lease or conditions that are not understood.

Here are some key Italian terms to keep in mind when looking for a rental in Italy:

Appartamento in affitto - Apartment for rent

Contratto di affitto - Rental contract

Arredato - Furnished

Bilocale - One bedroom

Due camere da letto - Two bedrooms

Monolocal - Studio

Servizi - Utilities

Edificio moderno - Modern building

FURNISHED OR UNFURNISHED

Whether or not you can find a furnished rental depends on the type of rental agreement you are looking for. Generally, long-term rentals (2 to 4-year leases) are unfurnished. You will have to think about furniture or moving your existing furniture in your budget. It is important to understand that in Italy, 'unfurnished' means totally devoid of everything but the walls! In fact, you probably won't have a refrigerator, stove or even lights. On the other hand, for a short-term lease (six months - one year) the property will probably come with furniture.

IS IT POSSIBLE TO GET AN APARTMENT WITHOUT INCOME OR WORK?

Whether you are able to get an apartment without a job depends heavily on where you live. Other EU residents are not required to have a job to get an apartment. However, most landlords require proof of income before they will allow you to move in, which in itself is normal. Non-EU residents will have to prove their legal residence in order to obtain an apartment. Although it is possible to obtain a visa as a student or in other circumstances, most visas are work visas and will only be issued to those who have obtained employment in Italy.

IS IT POSSIBLE TO NEGOTIATE THE RENT WITH THE OWNER?

Yes, and actually it's a good idea to do so. Since most rentals are from private landlords, their prices are usually slightly negotiable and they are less likely to be as inflexible as a rental agency. That being said, your real estate agent or a 'friend' in the area will have a much better chance of negotiating with the locals than you will. Italians tend to raise the price of rent for expatriates, as in other countries, because they are thought to have larger budgets. Having local knowledge works in your favor.

RULES FOR RENTING IN ITALY

In general, tenants have the same rights and duties in Italy as in other European countries. The landlord must generally approve all cosmetic improvements or alterations in advance and tenants must not damage the apartment, do anything illegal inside it or disturb the peace of their neighbors.

The owners reserve the right to remove a tenant if it is proven that he/she is destructive, disruptive or uses the apartment illegally. Since the apartments are mainly rented directly by their owners, the rules for subletting vary from one apartment to another. If you wish to sublet your apartment or part of it, Lisbob advises you to discuss this beforehand.

CONTRACTS, SECURITY DEPOSITS AND CHARGES

There are three types of lease contracts legally recognized in Italy, which vary according to the duration of the lease:
- Temporary, for stays up to 18 months;
- The 3 + 2 contracts are for a period of three years, with the possibility of renewal for two additional years;
- The 4 + 4 contracts are for four years and can be renewed for an additional four years.

The exact content of your rental agreement in Italy will vary from apartment to apartment, but by law it must contain at least the following information:

• Full name and address of owner;

• How much you will pay in rent and any anticipated changes to that amount: The amount of rent can be negotiated directly with the owner. As a general rule in Italy, the rent must be paid within the first seven days of the month, and the landlord cannot demand more than one month's rent in advance.

Regarding the method of payment, it is possible to pay the rent in cash or by bank transfer, but in all cases the landlord must provide a receipt.

• Deposit amount: The security deposit corresponds to the rental amount, i.e. one month's rent. The tenant must provide the deposit in cash and it will be returned to him at the end of the rental agreement provided that the property is returned in good condition in which case the deposit will not be returned. It is important to know that the owner cannot keep the deposit, which must be sent to the organization designated by each autonomous community.

In addition to the deposit, the landlord is entitled to request other guarantees, such as a guarantor or an insurance policy in case of loss of employment or income.

• Conditions to terminate your contract early;

• Conditions for the landlord to terminate your contract early

In Italy, it is the tenant's responsibility to pay all charges and certain taxes. These include:

- Garbage Collection Service;
- Gas;
- Electricity;
- Cable;
- Internet/Wifi;
- Television tax (if you own a television)

WHAT DOCUMENTS OR REQUIREMENTS ARE THERE FOR LEASING?

Renting an apartment in Italy can be a lot of paperwork as landlords are very careful to protect themselves when renting out their properties, and that's normal. It is best to have your agent or broker take care of everything for you, aside from signing your lease, of course.

IS IT POSSIBLE TO PAY BILLS FROM ABROAD?

Most Italian landlords will ask for a bank transfer or give you the option to pay via an online payment gateway. In both cases, you should be able to use your foreign bank. However, for tax reasons, it may be advisable to pay your rent from an Italian bank in order to keep track of your payments.

WHAT ARE THE BEST SITES TO FIND AN ACCOMMODATION?

Here are some good sites to start your search for a rental apartment in Italy:
- Subito;
- Idealista;
- Kijiji;
- Mioaffito.

If you are looking for a room in a shared apartment then you can also consult the following sites:
- Uniplaces;
- Spot-a-home
- Roomster;
- Erasmusu.

WHAT PRECAUTIONS SHOULD I TAKE TO AVOID BEING SCAMMED?

As in all countries, there are unfortunately people with bad intentions. When you don't know the Italian language or the rules of renting, it is normal and important to take precautions. Although scammers change their tactics every day, there are some rules to keep in mind so you don't lose your money:
- Never pay the owner in cash before signing the rental agreement. Having a record of a wire or

transfer is the key to getting your money back if it is stolen.

- Never agree to send money to a landlord you have never met. It may seem obvious but some people still fall into the trap and see their money go down the drain.
- Never allow your new landlord to mail your keys. This is far too great a risk.
- Try to confirm that the landlord is the owner of the apartment or make sure that the person has the right to sublet the apartment or house before agreeing to sign a document.

With this, you are ready to start your search for a rental in Italy. Good luck!

SCHOOL AND EDUCATION SYSTEM

Every school system is different depending on the country you live in and for many expatriates it is not easy to understand how the Italian school and education system works. From kindergarten to university, through high school and college, Italy has its own characteristics that should be known in order to best prepare your project. I'm Lisbob, your expat assistant, and I'm going to tell you all about the school and education system in Italy.

STRUCTURE OF THE ITALIAN SCHOOL SYSTEM

Italian schools can be

- Public: funded by the state
- Private: funded by tuition fees, i.e. money paid by students

The academic programs of these two types of schools follow the regulations of the Ministry of Education, University and Research (MIUR).

KINDERGARTEN

Attendance at this school is not compulsory (parents may decide to enroll their children as needed), and it is divided into:

- Asilo nido (kindergarten): attended by children from 0 to 3 years
- Scuola materna (pre-school): attended by children from 3 to 6 years old

From the age of 6 to 16, school attendance becomes compulsory, as established by law, and the child then enters the scuola dell'obbligo (compulsory education), which begins with elementary school.

ELEMENTARY SCHOOL

The elementary school is attended by students from 6 to 11 years old: the curriculum lasts 5 years in total. During these years, children learn to write, read and count. They learn about history, geography, mathematics, Italian grammar, science, music and physical education and, for the past few years, also English and computer science. Some schools offer religion courses that are optional.

MIDDLE SCHOOL

This new compulsory stage lasts 3 years and concerns all children from 11 to 13 years old. During this period, the students study the different subjects studied in elementary school, and at the end of this period, they must take the esame di terza media (equivalent to GCSE), composed of:

- Written Italian test;
- Written Mathematics Test;
- Written Language Test;
- An oral exam that consists of the presentation of a work on a specific theme including all the subjects studied.

If the 'GCSE' is validated, then the student can move on to the next level: high school.

HIGH SCHOOL

This stage lasts 5 years and is for students between 14 and 19 years old. However, from the age of 16, children have the possibility to abandon their studies.

Students can choose from 3 types of high schools depending on their goals:

LICEO: it offers a more theoretical and university-oriented training and, depending on the subjects studied, it can be of different types:

- Classico (Grammar) (Latin, Greek and Italian);
- Scientifico (Scientific) (Mathematics, Physics and Science);
- Linguistique (Language) (English and foreign languages);
- Tecnologico (Technology) (IT);
- Artisto (Artistic) (art);
- Musicale (Music).

VOCATIONAL TECHNICAL HIGH SCHOOL: in this type of
school, in addition to the common subjects, students can acquire practical and technical skills, adapted to entry into the job market, in sectors such as

- Economy;
- Tourism;
- Technology;
- Agriculture;
- Health.

ITF (VOCATIONAL EDUCATION AND TRAINING) in this
type of school, students acquire practical and professional skills. Studies at these schools focus on jobs such as

- Plumber;
- Electrician;
- Hairdresser;

- Beautician...

At the end of high school, the student must take another exam called *esame di maturità* (graduation exam, equivalent to the international baccalaureate). This test consists of 3 written tests and 1 oral exam, and in case of success a degree is issued, which allows access to university and higher studies.

UNIVERSITY

The Italian university curriculum is divided into three cycles.

FIRST CYCLE: Called *'laurea triennale'*, this cycle lasts 3 years. It is the equivalent of the bachelor's degree. There is a wide and diverse selection of Italian universities such as

- Scientific departments (Mathematics, Physics, Astrophysics, Chemistry...);
- Faculty of Humanities (Literature, Philosophy, Foreign Languages, Cultural Heritage...);
- Technical faculties (Architecture, Engineering, Economics...).

SECOND CYCLE: Also called *'laurea magistrale'* or *'specialistica'* (second level degree), this cycle usually lasts

2 years and is the continuation of the first cycle to ensure students a higher level of specialization. However, there are courses (Faculty of Law, Faculty of Pharmacy, Civil Engineering, Architecture, etc.) that last 5 years (6 years in the case of the medical school) and are called '*Corsi di Laurea a ciclo unico*' (single-cycle diploma courses).

THIRD CYCLE: this program is dedicated to the most ambitious students and includes:

> - Master's degree: these are generally short courses that offer the possibility (for those interested) of going into greater depth on specific aspects of the subject studied during the first two cycles.

> - PhD: these are theoretical courses, ideal for those who wish to pursue a career in academia or research.

HOW TO OBTAIN A DIPLOMA EQUIVALENCE AND HAVE YOUR SKILLS RECOGNIZED IN ITALY?

When you decide to live and work in Italy, it is important to know how to have your diplomas recognized and how to obtain an equivalence of skills. The European Union allows the free movement of citizens since its creation in 1993: this means that you also have, theoretically, the right to practice your profession in each member country. However, as you can imagine, theory is simpler than practice. In fact, there are diplomas, professions and skills that may not be recognized in Italy, or that require steps to be taken in order to have them recognized and obtain equivalence. If you wish to work in Italy, the question of validation of your diplomas will certainly arise. Because it is important to be able to prove to your future employer or your clients that you have the necessary knowledge, Lisbob has gathered for you the essentials on the recognition of diplomas and the equivalence of skills in Italy. How to obtain a diploma equivalence and have your skills recognized in Italy? What are the steps to take and the organizations to contact to have your diploma recognized? Let me tell you all about applying for and obtaining equivalence of diplomas and recognition of skills in Italy.

CONCEPT OF RECOGNITION AND EQUIVALENCE OF DIPLOMAS IN ITALY

Since the ratification of the Lisbon Convention, the concepts of recognition and equivalence of diplomas and training have been introduced in Italy. Before starting any evaluation procedure to have your foreign diploma recognized, it is therefore essential to know the purpose and objective for which recognition is requested from the Italian educational and university system. Among other things, it is necessary to take into account the different procedures in force in Italian legislation and the different bodies responsible for this type of request.

The answer to this question will indicate the most appropriate procedure and the authority responsible for carrying out this request. It is important to ask yourself beforehand what the purpose of the request for diploma equivalence is: whether it is to work, study, obtain a diploma or other. The applicant risks losing time in longer and more complicated procedures that may even result in the cancellation of the application for recognition of the diploma, all because of poor preparation.

In order to **enroll in a university program, a competitive examination or a doctorate,** foreign citizens and nationals with a university or professional degree obtained outside Italy can request official recognition from the Italian authorities. Professional diplomas are subject to the same regime. Further information can be obtained from CIMEA, the Information Centre on Mobility and Academic

Equivalence (*Centro di Informazione sulla Mobilità e le Equivalenze Accademiche*).

The equivalence or homologation of diploma and competence is an academic certificate that is based on the recognition and validation of a higher education degree. This equivalence is granted by the Italian universities, which make their decisions on a case-by-case basis. The objective is to **verify that a foreign degree corresponds exactly in detail to a similar degree from an Italian university**. If your degree does not have an equivalent in Italy, then it will be difficult to get it recognized.

HOW DO I APPLY FOR A DIPLOMA EQUIVALENCE IN ITALY?

In order to apply for a diploma equivalence in Italy, it is important to be well prepared and to present your application in the best possible way and directly to the competent Italian authorities and universities in order to lose as little time as possible and above all to optimize your chances of having your application accepted.

There are also different grades for academic positions in Italy. You can download the complete list of recognition and correspondence of academic degrees in Italy with all other countries on the website of the Italian Ministry of Education.

Each request must be sent and submitted to the University administration in charge of equivalencies that concern your degree or skills.

Once the right authority or university has been found, you must apply by submitting various forms and documents. If you are already officially living in Italy, you can submit your application directly in person. If you live abroad or are not yet an official resident of Italy, you must submit your application to the Italian Embassy or Consulate in your country before the date set by the Italian Ministry of Education, University and Research (MUIR).
In order to be complete and accepted, a request for equivalence of a diploma in Italy must include certain elements.

List of documents to be presented for a diploma equivalence in Italy:
- Application form to the University Dean;
- Original university degree in question;
- 3 passport photos;
- Original analytical certificate of university examinations issued by the university containing all details (dates, places, conditions);
- List and details of courses taken for each exam;
- The original school certificate that allowed you to be admitted to the university where you obtained your diploma. Now you know everything about how to obtain a diploma equivalence and have your skills recognized in Italy.

ALL THE DIFFERENT TYPES OF EMPLOYMENT CONTRACTS

When deciding to live and work in Italy, it is important to know the regulations in place regarding employment contracts. Although Italian labor law is similar to that of other European countries, the Italian legislation differs in certain points, even more since the recent modifications made to the Italian Labor Code. There are currently 7 different employment contracts in Italy, each with its own modalities and particularities, which are set out in the national collective agreements (contratti collectivi nazionali di lavoro, CCNL). An employment contract can be oral or written, but Lisbob obviously advises to make every effort to have a written contract. What are the characteristics of employment contracts in Italian law? What are the different employment contracts in Italy? Lisbob, your expat assistant in Italy, is going to tell you everything about Italian labor law in terms of contracts.

PERMANENT CONTRACT (CONTRATTO A TEMPO INDETERMINATO)

This is the equivalent of a permanent or open-ended contract. In Italy, the permanent contract is a classic contract, without an end date. There is a trial period during which either party can terminate the contract without having to give notice.

Although the length of the trial period is set by collective agreements, Italian law provides for a maximum duration of six months for the trial period of managers and first-class employees. Regarding permanent contracts for other employee categories, Italy sets a limit of 3 months. Once the period is over, the hiring becomes final.

For the employee, the new Italian legislation brings a novelty. Indeed, the law now provides that the employee may be assigned to any job at the same classification level, provided that the new job falls within the same category. Concretely, what changes is that from now on the worker can be assigned by his employer tasks not only equivalent to his professional field but also to others. It becomes legal for employers to allocate their employees to less important tasks.

On the employer's side, the new hiring bonus introduced in 2020 grants a 50% exemption from employer contributions for a period of 3 years for permanent contracts.

FIXED-TERM CONTRACT (CONTRATO A TERMINE)

As in other countries, Italy offers the possibility of establishing fixed-term contracts. A fixed-term contract may be part-time or full-time and have an end date. The duration of a fixed-term contract in Italy may not exceed 3 years.

Once expired, the fixed-term contract can only be renewed once for a period that cannot exceed the duration of the initial contract. Therefore, the total duration of the contracts must not exceed three years. For example, if the initial fixed-term contract has a duration of 3 years, then it is not possible to renew it. It will have to be transformed into a permanent contract.

The new Italian legislation brings simplification on the employer's side. Indeed, it is no longer mandatory for the company to justify the use of a fixed-term contract of less than 12 months. With this new feature, employers no longer have to explain why they need an employee for a specific time only.
In Italy, companies cannot have more than 20% of their employees on fixed-term contracts. For example, if a company has 5 employees, it can only have one on a fixed-term contract.

INTERIM CONTRACT (LAVORO INTERINALE)

In Italy, the interim contract is often an interesting opportunity for a first contact with the company since it allows the company to benefit temporarily from the work, without assuming all the costs related to the establishment of an employment relationship.

Unlike hiring directly with the company, the signing of an interim employment contract is tripartite. It links a temporary employment agency (or interim) with an employer and an employee. Unlike a fixed-term contract, the period of a temporary contract can be extended up to four times and the total duration cannot exceed 24 months. Beyond that, the contract must be requalified as a permanent contract.

In Italy, the employee must be informed of the extension of his temporary contract five days before the end date. Contract extensions must be formalized in writing and with the consent of the employee.

As in other European countries, Italy offers an apprenticeship contract. This type of contract is similar to the apprenticeship contract that exists in other countries. It mainly concerns Italians between 18 and 29 years old and can be carried out in any type of company. However, there is no age limit for an apprenticeship contract.

The duration of the apprenticeship contract is set between 24 and 72 months and must include a minimum of 120 hours of annual training.

Beneficiaries of an apprenticeship contract in Italy have the right to receive a salary. The amount of the latter increases gradually until it reaches that of a skilled worker.

COLLABORATION CONTRACT (COLLABORAZIONE COORDINATA E CONTINUATIVA)

This contract is a specificity of the Italian labor law. The collaboration contract, also called 'co-co-co' in Italian, is a form of contract that is becoming more and more widespread in Italy because it allows employers to reduce labor costs.

This contract is not a salaried job (dependenti) nor a self-employed job (indipendenti). The 'co-co-co' worker works in full autonomy and has no managerial organization.

The Italian law therefore speaks of a 'coordinated' and 'continuous' collaboration between the worker and the company, hence the term co-co-co. The worker decides autonomously when and how to carry out the orders he receives from the company he is contracted by.

PART-TIME WORK CONTRACT (LAVORO PART-TIME)

A part-time contract is not really a separate type of contract. It is the opposite of full-time work and must be formalized in writing. It establishes a working relationship with reduced hours, that is to say, less than 40 hours per week (legal working hours) and for periods predefined in advance.

This type of contract concerns the majority of students who work in addition to their studies. Please note that in Italy the minimum legal age to work is 16. Part-time workers shall not be discriminated against as compared to full-time workers with respect to their compensation and regulatory treatment.

Thus, the hourly wage and paid vacations are the same as those of a full-time worker, in proportion to the time worked.

In order to facilitate professional integration, Italy offers the integration work contract. The integration contract is a vocational training contract for young people aged 16 to 32. It is a fixed-term contract with a duration of between 1 and 2 years. This type of contract cannot be renewed and must include 20 to 140 hours of training.

Nevertheless, in the last few years, integration contracts have been used less and less in private companies, as they offer little advantages for the employer.

ITALIAN PUBLIC AND PRIVATE HEALTH SYSTEMS

When expatriating to Italy, it is important to be aware of the rules and customs concerning the Italian public and private health care systems. The Italian public health system is called *Servizio Sanitario Nazionale* (SSN) and it ranks 22nd in Europe, about ten places behind France. Expatriates in Italy will be able to choose between two types of health plans: the public health system, *Assicurazione Generale Obbligatoria* (AGO), or to complement it with a private health insurance. The quality of treatment and waiting times in the Italian public health system vary greatly from one region to another, which is why many expatriates choose to supplement their health coverage with private insurance. What are the characteristics of the health care systems in Italy? What are the differences between public and private health care systems? Lisbob, your expat assistant in Italy, answers all your questions on how to be treated and how to stay healthy.

PUBLIC HEALTH SYSTEM, SSN

The Italian health care system, the *Servizio Sanitario Nazionale* (SSN), is managed at the regional level and financed by the residents through taxes. Basic care is provided in local health units, formerly called USL for *Unità Sanitaria Locale*. From now on, the name of these centers will vary from one region to another: *Azienda Sanitaria Locale* (ASL), *Azienda Unità Sanitaria Locale* (AUSL) or *Azienda USL*, *Azienda Sanitaria Provinciale* (ASP), etc. At the national level, we usually call it ASL.

The care is provided by doctors who are either civil servants or private practitioners, but all of them have a contract. The insured person is free to choose the general practitioner, but a specialist can only be consulted with a prescription from the general practitioner. Hospitalization is free of charge in approved establishments but can only be done on the prescription of a general practitioner or a specialist. Of course, in case of emergency, it is possible to go directly to the hospital.

HOW TO ACCESS THIS SERVICE

In order to benefit from the Italian health care system, you must register with the SSN. The first step is to go to the local health administration or *Unità Sanitaria Locale* of your place of residence. Each insured person will obtain a health card or *Tessera Sanitaria*.

COVERAGE AND LIMITATIONS

The Italian health care system offers universal coverage similar to that offered by the French social security system, for example. However, the Italian health care system has a number of weaknesses that are important to know and consider before moving to Italy.

The Italian SSN covers

- General medical and dental care (some medical certificates are subject to fees) from registered practitioners;
- Treatment by registered specialists (with a minimum contribution of 34 euros);
- Hospital care in approved facilities;
- Prescription drugs with a minimum contribution of 3.10 euros per prescription (be careful because some drugs are not reimbursed at all);
- Partial coverage of certain services (prostheses, cures, laboratory tests, orthopedic care, etc.).

Care is provided at regional health centers or by doctors licensed by the NHS. The insured has the possibility to choose his or her initial general practitioner and may change once a year at the most. If another doctor is chosen then the insured will not be reimbursed. There are public clinics and private establishments that offer specialized care, particularly dental and orthopedic care.

At first glance, the Italian public health system seems to be pretty good. Nevertheless it has a number of negative points such as

- It is only possible to obtain a consultation with a specialist after a consultation with a general practitioner, thus lengthening the time required;
- The insured can only choose a contracted practitioner, which can be restrictive;
- Except for emergencies, admission to the hospital is by prescription from a general practitioner or a specialist under contract;
- Waiting times in the public sector can be very long;
- Due to the decentralization of the Italian health system, there are many inequalities between regions in terms of access and quality of care. Some hospitals are below the average quality standards (richer North and poorer South);
- The care is not entirely free of charge and you will be asked to pay a minimum fee for each service or medication.

For all these reasons, a growing number of expatriates are using the private health care system as a complement or alternative to the public system.

PRIVATE HEALTH SYSTEM

The private medical sector is highly developed in Italy. It is similar to what can be found in other European countries. In Italy, this private health care system makes it possible to deal with regional disparities and their consequences. As previously mentioned, the southern regions of Italy, including Sardinia, are the least well equipped in terms of quality of care. Many patients choose to seek treatment in the northern regions of the country, which considerably lengthens the waiting lists.

Choosing private health insurance will help you avoid waiting lists and access better quality care. Also, if you wish to visit a private specialist who is not covered by a convention, it will be very expensive: between 60 and 80 euros for a general practitioner and up to 150 euros for a specialist. A private health insurance plan will allow you to face this type of expense and to choose your practitioner in all serenity.

Another important point is hospitalization. If it is fully covered by the Italian public health system, you will have to pay for everything else, such as comfort and services. If you prefer to have a room to yourself, or to have a telephone, it is important to have a complementary private health insurance. The amount of your health insurance premiums will depend on the benefits you wish to receive as well as your level of risk (age, medical history, profession, hobbies), nothing too out of the ordinary.

MOVING: PREPARATION, PROCEDURES AND PRECAUTIONS

Have you finally made the decision to go live abroad? Your expatriation will necessarily go through the moving box. Leaving your country and moving to Italy can become a headache if you don't prepare well and if you don't know which trusted carrier to turn to. The organization of a move to Italy must be done with preparation and taking certain precautions. How to prepare for your move? What precautions should be taken when moving to Italy? I will tell you everything to move serenely to Italy.

OPTIONS AVAILABLE

There are different ways to move to Italy. Expatriation is not an easy task and moving often represents the link between old and new life. It is common to use professional international carriers to move your furniture, boxes, belongings and even vehicles to Italy. This first option is a priori one of the safest, even if it can be expensive and if the quality of the service will depend on the carrier chosen. I strongly recommend that you go through trusted professionals for your move.

Another possibility is to rent a van or van yourself. In this case you must rent the vehicle, load your belongings, furniture and others, and travel to Italy. There are usually franchises present in both countries and you will be able to drop off the vehicle in Italy. This solution is obviously less expensive, but it can be more complicated and exhausting. Packing, loading, transport, journey, unloading and assembly: you have to manage everything.

With your best friends and courage this solution can be attractive, but if the movers are professionals, it is because there is a reason: it is a real job that you do not fully master. There is a wide range of carriers for your move to Italy on the internet, but I can help you receive several proposals from quality carriers. In addition, the company in charge of your move to Italy will take care of the administrative procedures to ensure that everything is in order, such as customs clearance operations.

CARRIER QUOTE: OBLIGATIONS AND PITFALLS TO AVOID

In order to best prepare your move to Italy, you must take many precautions, especially during the quote stage. Your part of the job is to list everything (everything!)

that needs to be moved. We insist on being as precise as possible: try to list all the objects to the nearest spoonful, as well as the category in which they fall. Do they need to be packed, only transported, or are they fragile goods that require special care? It must also be specified whether the dismantling or packaging of certain objects is necessary. So, you already prepare your move to Italy in the most optimal way. This allows you to take stock of the situation and above all to send the right information to the carrier.

It is very important or even essential to draw up a document called the declaration of value. This document makes it possible to fix, in the event of loss or damage to your goods during the delivery of the carrier, financial compensation according to the damage suffered. It is up to you to complete it, specifying the overall value of your goods to be transported as well as the value of certain special goods whose unit value could exceed the contractual value limit per item. Without this document it will not be possible for the carrier to establish an estimate for your move to Italy. Be careful not to underestimate this document and the value of your goods to be transported because it is often a point of contention in the event of damage suffered during your move.

Once all this information has been transmitted, the mover will be able and must provide you with the most precise estimate possible, using the data that you have sent to him. The carrier's quote should include:
- Volume to be moved (usually expressed in cubic meters);

- Type of transport (truck, boat, rail, plane);
- Carrier services (packing/unpacking, disassembly/assembly, transport);
- Departure address/place of collection of the goods;
- Final address of arrival in Italy;
- Finally, the most important: the price.

I obviously advise you to request several quotes from different carriers in order to be able to compare the different offers and services. You can go to the Moving page on Lisbob.net to receive several quotes. My partners have been selected with the greatest care. You can of course read the various reviews and opinions of previous customers. All you have to do is choose the carrier that seems most suitable for your move to Italy.

THE IMPORTANCE OF DAMAGE INSURANCE

In most cases, damage and damage insurance will be offered to you by the carrier in charge of your move to Italy. If this is not the case, I strongly advise you to take out one. Indeed, this insurance covers any damage and damage during your move and transport. We informed you just before of the declaration of value: it is this amount which is insured.

Once again it is more than recommended to subscribe to it because even with the most careful carrier and during long journeys, you are not immune to slight damage to your furniture or your belongings. So thanks to this insurance you will be covered and this will allow you to be compensated.

Be careful because some carriers will tell you that your goods are insured without providing you with proof. This technique allows the mover to raise the bill, without offering any real insurance on your property. It is imperative that the carrier issues you the insurance certificate for your move to Italy. The cost of this damage insurance is calculated according to the declaration of value. The higher it is, the higher the cost of insurance will be.

RULES TO KNOW ABOUT PAYMENT AND DELIVERY

When you move to Italy it is normal to pay the cost to the carrier in several instalments. You pay a first part when loading your goods and business and the rest is due on delivery of these. This is of course not a universal rule because you can find other arrangements with the carrier in charge of your move to Italy, in particular depending on the volumes transported. There are rules to respect with your carrier in charge of your move to Italy. Indeed during loading and delivery it is mandatory to sign a "consignment note". It is by signing this document that you give your agreement to the carrier to begin the move and also at the very end of it.

This letter includes the information you have agreed on with the mover:

- Terms of the established contract
- Total volume transported (m3)
- Client name
- Transport company
- Mode of transport (road, plane, train)
- Loading and delivery address

It is essential for you to carefully check your belongings and goods upon delivery before signing the "consignment note". Once signed, you will no longer be able to claim any damage or damage that your property may have suffered during the move to Italy.

THE DELIVERY OF YOUR GOODS

It's D-Day: your goods are dismantled, packed and loaded. You are moving to Italy! It is up to you to tell the carrier the departure time and arrival date. You can also plan the route that will be taken by your goods if you ever travel at the same time. Be careful because some carriers do not deliver to the final address, but only to a collection point. In this case, you will have to collect your goods at a collection point and then transfer them to your home, obviously at your expense. Once your belongings have been received and unpacked, check that everything is present and in good condition.

HOW AND WHY TO REGISTER YOUR VEHICLE

Registering your car when you decide to move to Italy can sometimes turn into a waste of time and a headache if you are not sufficiently prepared. In order to import and register your vehicle in Italy, you will have to follow certain procedures and provide a list of documents and forms, pay fees and taxes and above all respect the deadlines. In fact, you have 6 months once installed in Italy to proceed to the change of plates of your foreign car. The subject comes up regularly on forums and help sites and the answers are sometimes unclear and often different on how and why to register your car in Italy. Is it compulsory to change your plates for Italian ones? What is the risk of not registering your vehicle on the roads of Italy? How much does it cost to import a car? How to register your car in Italy? I'm going to explain everything about this registration process that can sometimes turn into a real administrative labyrinth.

1. CANCEL THE REGISTRATION IN THE COUNTRY OF ORIGIN

The first step in registering your car in Italy is to simply cancel the existing registration in your country of origin. To do this, you must contact the relevant traffic authorities and you will be given a certificate of cancellation of registration in order to continue the process.

2. OBTAIN A CERTIFIED TRANSLATION OF DOCUMENTS INTO ITALIAN

In order to register your car in Italy, you will first need to request and obtain a certified translation of all the documents that are in French into Italian. Your grey card, the purchase invoice and the technical data sheet. It is mandatory to go through a certified Italian translator in order for the documents to be accepted to register your car.

3. OBTAIN THE EUROPEAN CERTIFICATE OF CONFORMITY (C.O.C.)

Called certificato di conformità in Italian, this document is like the identity card of the vehicle imported in Italy. It is essential to pass the technical inspection and must be requested directly from the manufacturer or the dealer of the vehicle. Do not hesitate to ask for this document long before your move to Italy: it can sometimes take several months to be issued and sent. Keep this document carefully in order to continue the procedures for registering your car in Italy. If you wish, Lisbob can order it directly from you: just go to our website or our application.

Example of a Certificate of Conformity:

4. PASS THE TECHNICAL INSPECTION

Once you have received the European Certificate of Conformity C.O.C., you can now take the technical inspection (controllo tecnico) of your vehicle. This car inspection is different from the usual control, and it is necessary to specify when you arrive that it is about the import and registration of a foreign car from another country of the EU. In Italy, technical inspection centers are called centro d'ispezione.

5. GO TO A MOTORIZZAZIONE CIVILE (UMC) OR ACI AUTOMOBILE CLUB D'ITALIA OFFICE.

The registration of a foreign car in Italy must be done with the competent authorities. It is important to prepare your file well and to gather all the necessary documents to change your license plates.

It is possible to get more information from the Motorizzazione Civile of your place of residence. You can consult the complete list of the offices of the 'Motorizzazione Civile' on their website,

City of Rome:
- via Salaria, 1045 - Tel: +39 06.81.691
urp.uprmnord@mit.gov.it
- via Fosso Acqua Acetosa Ostiense, 9 - Tel: +39 06.50.28.81 - urp.uprmsud@mit.gov.it
- via delle Cince, 28 - Tel: +39 06.23.18.02.10

City of Milan:
- via Cilea, 119 - Tel: +39 02.35.3790.01
urp_tecn.upmi@mit.gov.it

City of Naples:
- via Argine, 422 - Tel: +39 081 591 1111

Here are the documents and forms to be provided:

- Certificate of cancellation of registration of the country of origin;
- Technical specification form signed and stamped by the manufacturer or an accredited distributor;
- Application for registration *(domanda di immatricolazione)* form TT2119
- Vehicle registration document and its certified translation into Italian; a permanent export certificate may be sufficient;
- Technical control certificate signed and stamped by the manufacturer or an accredited distributor, with a certified translation into Italian.

The TT2119 form, which is essential for registering your car, is available on the Motorizzazione Civile website.

6. CHANGE YOUR LICENSE PLATES

With your precious Italian car registration certificate, you can now go to a garage to change your foreign license plates to Italian ones.

7. INSURING YOUR VEHICLE

The last step in order to drive safely and legally in Italy is, of course, to insure your vehicle. With your Italian grey card and your identity card, you can go to your insurer to subscribe to the car insurance that suits you best.

IS IT MANDATORY TO REGISTER YOUR CAR IN ITALY?

All European and non-European citizens who decide to live and settle in Italy *(domanda di residenza)* have a period of 60 days to proceed with the registration of the vehicle in Italy, change of license plates and car registration. The administrative penalties for failure to register a car in Italy can range from a fine of 712 to 2900 euros. In extreme cases, the authorities can impose an immediate stop of the vehicle. Lisbob advises you to start the process as soon as possible or to let professionals take care of it.

HOW TO BUY OR SELL A CAR

If you decide to buy or sell a vehicle in Italy, it will be important to know the rules and steps to follow. Also, there are many documents and proofs to provide for the buyer and the seller so that the transaction is done properly whether the car is new or used. In order to help you avoid being fooled, I am Lisbob, the expat assistant, and I will tell you how to buy or sell a car in Italy, whether it's new or second-hand.

BUYING A NEW CAR

This is the simplest solution but usually the most expensive: buying a new vehicle. Dealers selling new cars in Italy will usually take care of all the necessary paperwork on behalf of the buyer. A specialized agency known as Agenzia di Pratiche Auto carries out this process. The cost is included in the price of the new vehicle.

To find a local Agenzie di Pratiche Auto, visit the home page and enter the name of the region and city (in Italian).

The following documents must be provided by the buyer:

- Certificate of Residence (Certificato di Residenza) (a non-resident cannot buy a car in Italy, except from a manufacturer and with special conditions);
- Italian tax number *(Codice Fiscale)*;
- Identification document: required for the registration of the vehicle with the Traffic Control Authority (Motorizzazione Civile) and for the registration of the bill of sale with the Motor Vehicle Office (Pubblico Registro Automobilistico or PRA) managed by the Italian Automobile Club (Automobile Club d'Italia or ACI)
- Insurance document. In Italy the insurance must be taken out before the purchase of the car. All motor vehicles in Italy must have insurance *(assicurazione)* for at least civil liability. Failure to have adequate insurance will result in a heavy fine or even confiscation of the vehicle.

BUYING A USED CAR

Buying a used car in Italy is a more complex procedure than buying a new car, as it means more steps and verifications on the part of the buyer.

An *Agenzie di Pratiche Auto* can help you with the paperwork, for a fee.

The *Pubblico Registro Automobilistico* (PRA) office of the Automobile Club d'Italia will also draw up all the necessary documents on behalf of the buyer, including having them signed before an Italian notary. It may be helpful to have someone who speaks Italian well enough to understand the documents.

Used cars can be purchased through dealerships or via a number of online second-hand websites.

LEGAL FORMALITIES

Here are the documents required for the transfer of ownership of a used car in Italy:
- Deed of Sale (*Atto di Vendita*)
- Vehicle documents *(Certificato di Proprietà)*
- Vehicle registration certificate *(Carta di Circolazione)*
- Certificate of residence *(Certificato di Residenza)* for EU citizens;
- Personal tax numbers of the buyer and seller *(Codice Fiscale)*;
- Copy of the residence permit *(Certificato di Residenza)* for non-EU citizens.

There is a 60-day period to register the change of ownership *(passaggio di proprietà)* and update the car's registration certificate.

If the registration of the change of ownership is not carried out within 60 days, the former owner remains the de facto owner of the car in the public registry of vehicles and will remain responsible for the non-payment of taxes, accidents caused or violations of the Highway Code (Codice della Strada).

Verify that the registration has been completed by the PRA by contacting the AIT and providing them with the car's license plate numbers.

CHECKS

Before buying a used car in Italy, it is essential to check:

- Mileage, engine, tires;
- Maintenance information *(tagliandi)*;
- Expiry date of the traffic tax certificate *(scadenza bollo)*;
- Vehicle registration certificate *(Carta di Circolazione)*.

It is also possible to carry out a more in-depth study of the vehicle, preferably with the help of a mechanic.

SELLING A USED CAR

LEGAL FORMALITIES

If you sell a car in Italy, either to a private buyer or to a dealer, a deed of sale *(Atto di Vendita)* must be drawn up by an Italian notary.

Here are the documents you need to provide as a seller:
- Certificate of ownership *(Certificato di Proprietà)*;
- Vehicle registration certificate *(Carta di Circolazione)*.

If the car is to be transferred to a dealer for resale, then a notary must be asked to draw up a sale authorization *(Procura a Vendere)*.

HOW TO SELL A CAR

Before putting the vehicle up for sale, it is important to ensure that the maintenance checks are up to date with the garage.

Used cars can be sold through a dealer, either as a standard sale or as a part exchange for another vehicle. There are also a number of online classifieds sites that offer cars for sale.

Potential buyers may wish to take the car for a test drive *(giro di prova)*. Always make sure the person has a driver's license and accompany them on the test drive. Be prepared to barter and set a minimum price in advance.

You now have all the information you need to buy or sell a car in Italy.

HOW TO GET A DRIVING LICENSE IN ITALY?

If you decide to move to Italy, you may also decide to take (or retake) your driving test. Less expensive, less time consuming and less complicated than in other countries, the Italian driving license is recognized throughout Europe. However, the language barrier can sometimes be an obstacle to take the plunge and learn to drive. In fact, even if the Italian traffic code is more or less the same as in other European countries, it is necessary to learn to drive like an Italian. The locals say 'He who knows how to drive in Rome knows how to drive anywhere in the world.' How much does a driving license cost in Italy? What are the steps to register and take the test? How to pass the Italian highway code exam? How do I take the practical driving test in Italy? Lisbob, your expat assistant in Italy, is going to tell you everything you need to know about how to get a driver's license in Italy.

CONDITIONS FOR TAKING THE DRIVING TEST

Before you start the process of taking the Italian driving test, it is important to check if it is possible for you to register. In fact, Italy imposes certain conditions on all those who wish to register and take the driving test.

Conditions to register for the driving license in Italy

- Be at least 18 years old;
- Have a Codice Fiscale;
- Be a resident in Italy.

If you do not meet these 3 conditions, you will not be able to register for the Italian driving test. Once you are sure you meet all the criteria, you can start the registration process.

PRICE

It costs about 800 - 850 euros all inclusive to get your Italian license. Yes, it is cheaper than in most countries and you will see that it is also simpler. Beware of hidden fees and delays. In fact, you have a time limit to pass the theoretical and practical tests of the Italian driving license. If you miss these deadlines, you will have to reapply and pay a new fee. Lisbob will come back to this point a little later.

REGISTRATION

Have you decided to take your **driving** test in Italy? Very interesting challenge! It may seem difficult or even impossible when you think you don't understand the language (let alone know how to drive), but it is easier to obtain in Italy than in most other countries. The first thing to do will be to choose your driving school, but the procedures can also be carried out at the nearest Motorizzazione Civile office. In this case it is possible to download the form directly in advance and fill it in to save time, by clicking here.

Your application for the Italian driving license must be complete and include a number of documents, forms and proofs in order to be accepted. In order to save time, Lisbob advises you to prepare your file and check it before going to a driving school or a Motorizzazione Civile office.

List of documents to register for the Italian driving license:

- Form TT2112 completed and signed;
- Identity document (original + photocopy);
- Codice Fiscale (original + photocopy);
- 2 identity photos;
- Medical certificate with photo less than 3 months old, with stamped paper worth 16 €. Please note that this medical certificate can only be issued by a certified doctor. You can consult the complete list by clicking here;
- Second medical declaration, issued by your general practitioner (original + photocopy)
- Certificate and proof of payment of the preprinted bulletins C/C 9001 and C/C 4028, worth €26.40 and €16 respectively. These bulletins can be found in the offices of the Motorizzazione or in the Italian post offices.

Once the application is completed and submitted to the appropriate authorities, you will be given a training booklet that will follow you throughout your training for the Italian driving test. From that moment on, you have 6 months to pass the theory test. Be careful because once the deadline has passed you will have to redo the procedures. Once the theoretical exam is passed, the deadline for taking the practical exam is 5 months.

THEORY COURSE AND EXAM

In order to obtain an Italian driving license, as in other European countries, each person who wishes to obtain a license must complete a theoretical part during which he or she will learn about the Italian traffic regulations and the habits and customs of drivers in Italy. Nothing very original, the Italian highway code is very similar to the one found elsewhere in Europe and the signs are also very similar and it will not be difficult to recognize them.

The test consists of 40 questions. The candidate should not make more than four errors, or a maximum of 10%. If the exam is not passed, then it is possible to retake it only 1 month after failing it, not before. Be careful because it will only be possible to retake it a second time. If you fail the Italian driving test a second time, you will have to submit a new application and pay all the fees again.

You can answer in any order you like, change the answer to a question. At the end of the 30 minutes, the system stops and the examiner calls you one by one to tell you the number of errors. Of the 40 questions, 35 are common sense and logical (always take the most 'safe' answer that involves the least amount of risk), and 5 require you to know the answer (or take a chance). Then you will only need to translate the few important words of the Italian driving vocabulary and traffic rules and you will be ready to learn to drive.

Did you pass the exam? Congratulations! From now on I will explain the driving.

LEARNING AND PRACTICAL DRIVING TEST

Learning to drive in Italy requires a minimum of 6 hours of driving in the presence of a professional and registered driving school instructor. The main topics covered during the driving lessons in Italy are urban driving, fast lane driving and night driving.

I remind you that the quality of learning depends greatly on the complicity between the instructor and the apprentice. So don't hesitate to ask for another instructor if you are not comfortable with yours. After each lesson, the instructor signs the learning booklet previously given by the competent authorities.

Regarding the language level, you will need to learn these few essential words:

- Sinistra (Left);
- Destra (Right);
- Dritto (Straight);
- Retromarcia (Reverse);
- Parco (Parking)

By mastering these few Italian words, you will understand 90% of what the instructor tells you to do. And for the remaining 10%, it will give you an additional opportunity to improve your Italian. You will be able to choose the date of the exam after a minimum of 6 hours with an instructor.

You receive the pink sheet (foglio rosa) when you take the practical exam. This document allows you to practice driving on Italian roads provided that you are accompanied by a person with a driving license for the category you are applying for, that it was obtained at least 10 years ago and that the license holder is under 65 years old. Please note that this document is valid for 6 months.

The practical exam can be taken at least one month after receiving the foglio rosa, the pink sheet. If you fail the exam, you will only be able to retake it once during the 6 months. If you are taking the Italian driving test for categories B or C, then it is mandatory to take the test with a car equipped with dual controls.

Is that all? Yes: no trick questions about speed limits while driving, no test to see if you know how to change a tire or check the oil level. As Lisbob told you, it is easier to get a driving license in Italy than in other countries.

If you pass the exam, congratulations! You automatically get the precious key to freedom: the Italian driving license. You will only be able to drive vehicles in the categories for which you have passed the test. The Italian license is called a *patente*. It is valid in all countries of the European Union and includes 20 points. It must be renewed every 10 years with a medical visit: this obligation increases to 5 years from 50 years old. Finally, the Italian driving license must be renewed every 3 years from the age of 70.

HOW TO OPEN A BANK ACCOUNT

Opening a bank account is one of the first administrative steps to take when moving to Italy. Regardless of your situation, it is quite simple to open an account in an Italian bank. The requirements and documents needed to open a bank account in Italy are similar to those found in other European countries. Beyond the simple fact of going to a bank branch, it is important to first choose the right Italian bank, adapted to expats, and then to be prepared for slightly different operating rules than elsewhere. In addition, the language barrier can be an obstacle in understanding how a bank account works in Italy. Which banks are suitable for expats? How do I open a bank account in Italy? Let me explain everything about opening an account in an Italian bank.

Italy is a country that has a banking system similar to what we can find in other European countries. In fact, the different types of bank accounts and cards are similar because Italy is a member of the European SEPA transaction system and VISA and MASTERCARD are widely used.

There are 2 types of bank accounts in Italy:
- Current account (conto corrente in Italian) allows you to carry out all daily banking operations;
- Savings account (conto di risparmio), but the interest in Italy is a little lower than in other countries.

Credit cards are the same as in other countries:
- Debit card (carta di debito)
- Credit card (carta di credito)

WHICH BANK TO CHOOSE

When it comes to choosing your bank in Italy, you will be spoilt for choice. It will depend on your needs and what you want from your bank. If you are looking to open your bank account in an online bank, in a worldwide presence or with facilities for professionals. Here are, in alphabetical order, the main banks in Italy:

- Banca d'Italia
- Banca di Roma
- Banca Popolare
- Banca di Brescia
- Monte dei Paschi di Siena
- Banque du Vatican
- Intesa Sanpaolo
- Unicredit

It is possible to compare the fees of different banks directly on the website of the Bank of Italy. It is important to know that bank fees are higher in Italy than elsewhere. Indeed, the 2008 crisis left some banks in difficulty. Although the crisis is over, it continues to cost Italian taxpayers money. You will have to be very careful when choosing your bank and card. In any case, Italian banks offer the same capital guarantees as other European countries, i.e. €100,000 per taxpayer.

Also as an expat, I strongly recommend that you also open a Revolut online account.

Opening a bank account in Italy allows you to domicile your income and benefit from banking services such as debit or credit cards, home loans or international transfers.

The bank account cannot be opened without Codice Fiscale in Italy. It is also necessary to present documents in order to open a bank account, such as
-    Identification: valid national identity card or

     passport;
-    Codice Fiscale;
-    Proof of address: electricity, water or telephone

     bill;
-    Proof of occupation: employment contract, pay

     slip.

It is usually necessary to pay money (about 100€) in order to open a bank account in Italy.

As an expat, it is sometimes difficult to find a bank that is convenient, online, inexpensive and expat-friendly. Lisbob strongly recommends Revolut Bank: a free Visa card and an IBAN in less than 5 minutes. In addition, you can benefit from travel insurance and fast transfers. In short, the best bank for expats.

Here is how to open a bank account in Italy:
1. Choose your bank
2. Submit the requested documents
3. Choose your bank account type
4. Sign the contracts

If you want to make it much simpler, you can (and Lisbob highly recommends it) open a bank account in 5 minutes with Revolut. You can open your bank account online and order your free Visa card.

Now you know everything about opening a bank account in Italy.

HOW TO APPLY FOR AND OBTAIN THE SPID

Italy is a country that has a reputation for lagging behind in modernizing and simplifying its bureaucracy. Slow, complicated, unreliable: feedback from experience makes it normal to be apprehensive about having to deal with it. Nevertheless, for a few years now, the situation has been evolving and there is the SPID, an online identification system that allows certain administrative procedures to be carried out remotely. The Public Digital Identity System (SPID) is becoming more and more widespread and is even mandatory for certain procedures. How do you ask for it and what is it for? I'm Lisbob, your expat assistant, and I'm going to tell you all about how to get your SPID in Italy.

WHAT IS THE PURPOSE OF THE ITALIAN SPID

The Public Digital Identity System (SPID) allows you to carry out administrative procedures online, without having to go anywhere. The pandemic has facilitated its use and it is now possible to do many things such as pay fines, fill out a tax return, request a civil status certificate or register a child at school. Pensioners are even required to use the SPID as it is mandatory to access the services of the Italian pension fund, the INPS.

In short, the SPID is an essential element for your daily life and as an expatriate you have every right to obtain one. This will save you time and travel.

HOW TO GET THE SPID

The first good news is that the SPID is a free process (in most cases) and can be done throughout Italy for people over 18 years old. This requires only one trip to validate your identity, but it is also possible to do it entirely online in some cases. The first step is to gather the complete file.

The following is a list of documents and items required to apply for the SPID:

- Valid identification;

- Tessera sanitaria;

- Codice Fiscale;

- E-mail address;

- Italian cell phone.

Once all the elements have been gathered, you must go to a recognized institution officially authorized to recognize your identity and provide the SPID. These establishments are usually public places such as town halls or post offices.

You can consult all the authorized establishments at this address   https://www.spid.gov.it/en/what-is-spid/how-to-activate-spid/the-pas-obtain-spid/

Then, you have to register on the website of the chosen SPID provider, following the steps below:
Fill in your personal data;
Create a SPID;
Perform identity recognition, choosing between free or paid methods offered by recognized institutions. It can be done in person (which requires travel) or online (via webcam).

The Italian SPID is issued almost instantly for applications made entirely online. Requests made in person are processed within 5 business days. Once obtained, the Italian SPID can be used immediately and is final. This will be valid for life and it is therefore advisable to keep your identifiers.

137

STEPS TO TAKE BEFORE LEAVING

That's it, you've finally decided to move to Italy. If this decision has been carefully thought out, the project that follows must also be well prepared in order to have a successful expatriation. Moving to another country is not just about packing your bags and it is important to respect many steps and procedures before leaving your country, otherwise you may experience unpleasant last-minute surprises. In order to motivate you and to help you in this fabulous project, I'm going to tell you everything about the steps to take before moving to Italy.

MORE THAN 6 MONTHS BEFORE DEPARTURE

Preparing for your expatriation starts well before your moving date, such as choosing which region to move to. Italy is a rich and varied country, and each region has very different traits.

☐ Learn about Italy: read specialized websites and expatriate blogs (such as Lisbob.net) and join social networking groups to get information about local life in different regions. Forums can be a good source of inspiration although the information is sometimes too old to be correct.

☐   You can also check out our YouTube channel, with lots of videos to motivate you in your project and explain several administrative procedures.

☐   Organize one or more stays in the country you have chosen, to visit the regions, cities or villages you like and choose your destination to settle in. Beware, the place you would like to be on vacation may not be the same place where you would like to spend the majority of your time. It can be useful to visit out of season to get a feel for 'normal' life.

☐   It is also possible to read our books in English, dedicated to expatriation and updated every year.

BETWEEN 3 AND 6 MONTHS BEFORE DEPARTURE

The excitement is building, and now it's time to take concrete steps for your project. We can't repeat it often enough, good preparation is the key to a successful expatriation.

☐   Start the rental search. Have you chosen your destination to settle down? You can now start your rental search. It is preferable to start with 2 to 4 weeks of tourist rental in order to get your bearings and to be able to do the research for the long term once on the spot. If you already have your NIE then you can already find a long-term rental property, but it will be complicated to make contracts and visit from a distance.

☐   Pets. Four-legged animals must also prepare their expatriation. In order to avoid unpleasant surprises, it is essential to inform yourself about the necessary vaccinations, the formalities to be completed before departure (import permits, quarantine...) as well as the conditions of transport if you take the plane. Do not forget to consult your veterinarian to prepare the health booklet or to update the microchip. We have an article on this subject.

☐ Find out about your vehicle registration. If you wish to import your current vehicle to Italy, then it is essential to find out about the procedures and taxes beforehand. You can contact an importer or a customs broker to find out the amount of this tax. If you have decided not to keep your car, put it up for sale and cancel your insurance.

☐ Current housing: it's time to send your notice to the landlord or to put your property up for sale or rent.

☐ Request several moving quotes. Moving is one of the most complicated steps in any expatriation project. Whether you have a few boxes or large pieces of furniture, it is important to choose the right international carrier. It is recommended to establish 3 quotes in order to compare the different offers, and especially to make sure that the insurance is well included.

☐ Check your identity documents. If necessary, you will have to renew your passport or your identity card if their validity is not sufficient to meet the requirements of your host country. The passport remains the best document for expatriation.

☐ Learn basic Italian. In order to integrate into your future host country, it is best to start learning basic

Italian. The written language is quite easy to understand because it is Latin, but we do not recommend listening to Italian to begin with. The pronunciation is easy to understand and to express. All our books include an English- Italian lexicon to familiarize you with the basics of the language.

BETWEEN 1 AND 3 MONTHS BEFORE DEPARTURE

☐ Bank: In order to avoid unpleasant surprises regarding fees and conditions, contact your current bank about money transfers as well as maintaining an account while being resident in Italy. Some banks have offices in both countries, which makes expatriation much easier.

☐ Health insurance. In order to join the Italian social security system free of charge, you will need to apply to your health insurance fund for the S1 form or the European Health Insurance Card (EHIC) if you continue to live in your home country for more than 6 months per year.

☐ Medical documents: gather and keep all important health-related documents: vaccination booklet, health booklet, blood type card, prescriptions, X-rays. You can scan them and put them in an online file to access them from anywhere.

☐ Car insurance. If you have decided to take your vehicle to Italy, then the rule is that you are insured by your current insurer for 3 months, extendable to 6 with written agreement. Beyond that, it is impossible to be insured and you will first have to register your vehicle in Italy in order to take out Italian car insurance.

☐ Cancel current contracts. It's time to cut your current contracts and notify the various services of your move abroad. This point is important because many expatriates forget this and end up paying for a contract they do not use. It may be advisable to keep your current cell phone plan as they are more expensive in Italy.

☐ Find out about the validity of your driver's license and if necessary, apply for an international driver's license. If you have a pink license (no expiry date) then you will need to exchange it within the first two years of your arrival. Otherwise, you will have to exchange it once its validity date has expired.

☐ Contact the carrier. It is important that the move be well prepared so that it goes smoothly. This is often a major source of stress, and it is important to get in touch with your carrier to find out about export clearance procedures and the rules for special items (furniture, jewelry, plants, food, etc.).

☐ Keep a photocopy of important documents: family record book, birth certificate, passport... You can also store these documents in digital format and send them to your email address to access them anywhere in the world.

LESS THAN A MONTH BEFORE DEPARTURE

It's the final stretch, the pressure is at its highest and the excitement is mixed with apprehension. If you have followed the above steps, then everything will go smoothly. One more effort and you will have realized your dream: living in Italy.

☐ Administration: it is now time to inform the administrations of your country of your departure to Italy, and to communicate your new address (if you already have a long-term property): tax office, pension funds, bank, post office, etc.

☐ Sorting out your belongings. It's time to pack your suitcases and boxes, to pack everything well and why not sort your things. You can donate clothes and objects in good condition that you no longer use or put them on sale online.

☐ If you already have your NIE, you can already subscribe online to the different services for your Italian home: electricity, gas, water, telephone, internet. These steps are simple and are done online, and you can notify your arrival date.

☐ Insurance: Whether it is health, home, car or life, it is important to establish different estimates and to cover yourself, even more so in a new country. You can contact a website like Inov'Expat, which will find the best quotes according to your criteria.

☐ Organize a farewell party. Indeed, an expatriation wouldn't really be complete without a moment with your loved ones and some tears. They can be a source of motivation for your project and you can be a source of inspiration for them. It's also a time to say goodbye to your neighborhood, your city and your region, before leaving for an adventure.

You now know the main steps and procedures to follow before your departure to Italy. Of course, each project is unique, and it will be important to take stock of the situation and see what issues need to be explored, such as taxation, investments or long-term care.

LEXICON

ENGLISH	ITALIANO
Basic	Di base
Hello	Buongiorno
How are you?	Come state ?
Very well thank you.	Molto bene grazie.
What is your name?	Come ti chiami ?
My name is	Mi chiamo
Nice to meet you.	Piacere di conoscerti.
Please	Per piacere
Thanks	grazie
Yes	sì
Nope	No
excuse me	Scusami
Goodbye	Arrivederci
I do not speak Italian	Io non parlo italiano
Do you speak English?	Parli inglese ?
Does anyone speak English?	Qualcuno parla inglese?
Help!	Aiuto !
Good morning)	Buongiorno
Hello afternoon)	Ciao
Good evening	buona serata
I don't understand	Non capisco

Could you repeat the question?	Potresti ripetere la domanda?

Temporality	Temporaneamente
Now	Adesso
Later	Dopo
Before	Prima
Next	Prossimo
Morning	La mattina
Afternoon / evening	Pomeriggio sera
This evening	Questa sera
The night	La notte
Days	Giorni
Year	Anno
Month	Mese
Today	Oggi
Yesterday	Ieri
tomorrow	Domani
This week	Questa settimana
Last week	La settimana scorsa
Next week	La prossima settimana
Monday	lunedì
Tuesday	martedì
Wednesday	Mercoledì
Thursday	Giovedì
Friday	venerdì
Saturday	il sabato

Sunday	Domenica

Transportation	Trasporto
I would like to go...	Vorrei andare...
Plane	Aereo
Boat	Barca
Taxi	Taxi
Train	Treno
Bus	Pulman
I would like to rent...	Vorrei affittare...
Car	Auto
Motorbike	Moto

Health / Emergencies	Salute / Emergenze
Call a doctor/ambulance	Chiama un medico/ambulanza
I hurt here	Ho fatto male qui
I do not feel very well	Non mi sento molto bene
I need to see a doctor.	Ho bisogno di vedere un dottore.
Help!	Aiuto !
Police	Polizia
Danger	Pericolo
I'm lost)	Mi sono perso)
Where is the hospital?	Dov'è l'ospedale?
Where are the toilets?	Dove sono i bagni ?
Social Security	Sicurezza sociale
Health center	Centro sanitario

Medical exams	Esami medici

Finance	Finanza
Tax Identification Number	Codice Fiscale
Taxpayer	Contribuente
Tax	Imposta
Pay	Paga
Invoice / Receipt	Fattura / Ricevuta
Bank	Banca
ATM card	Bancomat
Credit card	Carta di credito
Fixed rate	Tasso fisso
Floating rate	Tasso variabile

Accommodation	Alloggio
Bedroom	Camera da letto
House	Casa
Apartment	Appartamento
To rent out	Affittare
To buy	Comperare
Sale	Vendere
Collocation (Share)	Collocazione (quota)
Credit	Credito
Guarantor	Garante
Tourist rental	Affitto turistico
Contract	Contrarre
Key	Chiave

Work & Business	Lavoro e affari
Freelancer	Libero professionista
Green receipt (invoice)	Scontrino verde (fattura)
Fixed-term contract	Contratto a tempo determinato
Holidays	Vacanza
Basket/meal voucher	Cestino/buono pasto
Company	Azienda
Company	Società
Accounting	Un ragioniere
Economy	Economia
Work	Lavoro
Boss	Capo
Employee	Dipendente
Conference	Conferenza
Results	Risultati
Mistake	Errore
Insurance	Assicurazione
Industry	Industria
Colleagues	Colleghi
Competitor	Concorrente
Performance	Prestazione
Negotiation	Negoziazione
Vendor	Fornitore
Compromise	Compromesso
Opportunity	Opportunità
Permanent contract	contratto a tempo indeterminato

Hobbies	Hobby
Travel	Viaggiare
Go to a concert	Andare ad un concerto
To go to the museum	Per andare al museo
Go jogging	Andare a correre
Play ball	Giocare a palla
Go to the gym	Vai in palestra
Play soccer	Giocare a calcio
To paint	Pitturare
Play sports	Fare sport
Cycling / bicycling	Ciclismo/bicicletta
Watch television	Guardare la televisione
Read a book	Leggere un libro
Read the newspaper	Leggere il giornale
Play guitar	Suonare la chitarra
Play the violin	suonare il violino
Play piano	Suonare il piano

Weather & Climate	Meteo e clima
Season	Stagione
Spring	Primavera
Summer	Estate
Fall	Autunno
Winter	Inverno
Sun	Sole
Moon	Luna
Star	Stella

Cloud	Nuvola
Wind	Il vento
Snow	Neve
Rain	Piovere
Heat	Calore
Cold	Freddo
Storm	Tempesta
Temperature	Temperatura
Tide	Marea
Haze	Nebbia

At the restaurant	Al ristorante
Do you have...	Devi...
Knife / fork / plate / spoon / glass	Coltello/forchetta/piatto/cucchiaio/bicchiere
I made a reservation on behalf of...	Ho effettuato una prenotazione per conto di...
I will need...	Io avrò bisogno...
I'll have this / this dish / cheese / dessert / coffee	Prenderò questo/questo piatto/formaggio/dolce/caffè
I would like... Please.	Vorrei... Per favore.
The bill please.	Il conto per favore.
Non-smoker, please.	Non fumatore, per favore.
Can I have a little more...	Posso avere un po' di più...
Can I have the menu?	Posso avere il menu ?
What do you have for drinks?	Cosa prendi da bere?

151

What's in this dish? / Is there... in this dish?	Cosa c'è in questo piatto? / C'è... in questo piatto?
A table for ... people.	Un tavolo per... persone.

At the hotel	Nell'albergo
Do you have rooms available?	Avete stanze disponibili?
I have a reservation in the name of...	Ho una prenotazione a nome di...
I would like to stay one more night.	Vorrei restare un'altra notte.
Is breakfast included?	La colazione è inclusa?
Where is the room located?	Dove si trova la stanza?
Can you take my luggage?	Puoi prendere il mio bagaglio?
What restaurant do you recommend?	Quale ristorante mi consigliate?
One bedroom..., please.	Una camera da letto..., per favore.
Is there... in this room?	C'è... in questa stanza?
Is there internet access?	C'è l'accesso a Internet?
Is there a baggage locker?	C'è un armadietto per i bagagli?

EMERGENCY PHONE NUMBERS

These free national emergency numbers are accessible from telephone booths, without using a phone card or money.

- Police (Carabinieri) 112
- General emergency (Soccorso pubblico di emergenza) 113
- Firefighters (Vigili del fuoco) 115
- Forest fire (Incendio boschivo) 1515
- Assistance in the event of car breakdown (Socorso Stradali) 116
- Ambulance/medical emergencies (Emergenza sanitaria) 118
- Pan-European emergencies 112

There are emergency phones every two kilometers on the autostrada (autostrada) which connect directly to the ACI (the Italian Automobile Club).

European SOS 112

The number 112 can be dialed to reach the emergency services - medical, fire and police - from anywhere in Europe. The operator connects the caller to the required emergency service. This pan-European emergency number, 112, can be called from any telephone (landline, payphone or mobile phone). Calls are free. It can be used for any life-threatening situation, including:

- Serious medical problems (accident, unconscious person, serious injuries, chest pain, epileptic seizure);
- Any type of fire (house, car);
- Life-threatening situations (crimes).

Other useful numbers

- Child Abuse Helpline Tel: 19696
- Prevention of abuse of women Tel. : 800 001 122
- Directory information (Informazioni elenco abbonati) Tel. : 12
- International operator (English speaking)
- (International information) Tel. : 170
- Freephone numbers (Numeri Verdi) prefix prefix 147 or 800

IN THE SAME COLLECTION

Made in United States
Troutdale, OR
10/24/2024

24115105R00090